WINNING A DAY AT A

WINNING A DAY AT A TIME

JOHN LUCAS
with
Joseph Moriarity

■ HAZELDEN®

Hazelden Educational Materials
Center City, Minnesota 55012-0176

©1994 by Hazelden Foundation
All Rights reserved. Published 1994
Printed in the United States of America
No portion of this publication may be reproduced in
any manner without the written permission of the publisher

Library of Congress Cataloging-in-Publication Data
Lucas, John (John H.)
  Winning a day at a time / John Lucas with Joseph Moriarity.
    p.   cm.
  ISBN 1-56838-028-3
  1. Lucas, John (John H.) 2. Basketball players—United States—Biography.
3. Basketball coaches—United States—Biography.
I. Moriarity, Joseph. II. Title.
GV884.L83A3 1994
796.323'092—dc20
[B]   94-26251
                                                                            CIP

Editor's note
    Hazelden Educational Materials offers a variety of information on chemical dependency and related areas. Our publications do not necessarily represent Hazelden's programs, nor do they officially speak for any Twelve Step organization.

CONTENTS

Prologue 1

Chapter 1 Hitting Bottom 5

Chapter 2 Early Childhood 15

Chapter 3 Junior and Senior High School 27

Chapter 4 University Years 43

Chapter 5 Pro Career 61

Chapter 6 Recovery 93

Chapter 7 Return to Basketball 113

Chapter 8 The Tropics 135

Chapter 9 Coach of the Spurs 147

Chapter 10 John Lucas Today 191

Epilogue George "Iceman" Gervin 211

To all my friends
whose last names
I'll never remember.

PROLOGUE

I first met Lloyd Daniels in an airport in Milwaukee, when he was playing in the Continental Basketball Association (CBA) a few years back. His coach, who introduced us there in the concourse, wanted me to meet Lloyd because he felt that Lloyd had the talent to play in the NBA. That's why Lloyd was in the CBA — it was a way to play ball and maybe make the right connection with an NBA scout or coach to get to the pros.

I knew Lloyd had had some trouble in his life, and he'd been kicked out of the University of Nevada Las Vegas before he even had a chance to play. I took one look at Lloyd and I knew his troubles weren't over yet. He was still using drugs. He wasn't even ashamed of it; he admitted it to me when I confronted him. I think he was even proud of it. So I pulled Lloyd over to the side and I said, "Hey, young fellow, you got to put it up. You got to, Lloyd, or else you not only won't play in the NBA, you'll be dead."

Lloyd Daniels, guard, San Antonio Spurs

> *Put it up! I didn't want to hear that shit. I'd been using for years. Where I grew up in Brooklyn, everybody's using. My mother died when I was three, and I started smoking marijuana with my uncle when I was ten. I figured, if he's going to*

smoke it, I'll smoke it with him just to keep it in the family.

Not long after I met Lucas in that airport, I was back in Brooklyn, doing some foolish shit. One day I got shot, right in front of my grandmother's house. The morning after I got out of the hospital, I got high again. I get shot, come out of the hospital, and go right back out and get high. That's how strong this disease is. I still didn't want to hear that "put it up" shit, but Lucas's words were still in the back of my mind because the stuff he was telling me seemed real. I guess I was finally at a point where I knew I had to do something. Forget about basketball. I knew my life wasn't going nowhere after being shot. Just like he said. Everyone's got to wake up some day, and after I came out of the hospital and got high again, I finally looked in the mirror. I said, "Hey, Lloyd, you got to stop. You're not going nowhere. It's just like running into a brick wall. You got to put it up."

About this same time, Lucas bought this team, the Miami Tropics [in the United States Basketball Association]. A guy I'd played for, Jim Price, was one of the Tropics' coaches. Price knew I was struggling trying to stay clean, so he called me and said, "Lloyd, I think you should call John Lucas and go down with him. He can help you." So I called John, and he gave me and my wife enough money to get us and our little Nissan down to Houston. When I got there, what he told me was this: "Lloyd, all you have to do is follow the program and do the work; I'll take care of the rest."

And he did. It's amazing how he was there for me. "Recovery's first, Lloyd," he would always say, because with John Lucas, recovery is first. What finally stopped me from using was that I looked at him and I thought, "Shoot, if he can do it, I can do it. He ain't no better than me. He's an addict just like me."

After I started getting better, John Lucas was calling NBA scouts, getting them to fly to Houston to see Lloyd Daniels to show them that I was clean, that I could stay clean off the court, that I had the talent to play, and that I was ready for the NBA. He was asking them to just give me a chance.

And here's how God worked. I came to the San Antonio Spurs when Jerry Tarkanian was head coach in the 1992-93 season. Tarkanian brought me in, and then he got fired about twenty games into the season. The night after they fired Tarkanian, we were all sitting in the locker room after a game with Houston, and the owner of the club at the time, Red McCombs, he comes in and says, "Guys, meet your new coach, John Lucas."

Whoever thought John Lucas would be Lloyd Daniels's coach! Especially after all I'd been through with him, being in the guy's program, going to meetings with him and all that! Here's another brother, your recovering brother, going to be your coach. It shows you how the Lord works. It was just amazing, and that's how I know, like they say, that I have a Higher Power. Playing for him is something else.

I know I've got to be grateful, especially a guy like me, because I've been shot and I came back from hell. I'm a miracle to be here and be clean. And John, he helped me see that. He helped me get to where I am today. You got to love the guy, you really do. I know that I couldn't be on this team if it wasn't for Lucas helping me get sober. I wouldn't even be playing ball. John Lucas is God-sent. The guy's been there — and he'll be there for you.

CHAPTER 1

HITTING BOTTOM

Just as Lloyd Daniels ignored me when I pulled him aside a few years ago in the airport and told him that he had to put it up, I was unwilling to put up my drug use for the first six years of my professional career. I had been addicted to and abusing myself with alcohol and cocaine since about 1978-79, my third year in the NBA. After three or four years of serious using, I was being urged by my friends, my wife, my sister, other players, former coaches — lots of people — to stop using.

Like Lloyd, I didn't want to hear nothing like that because I didn't think I even had a problem. On the rare occasions when I let myself think that maybe I needed to make some changes, I just told myself that I'd simply make up my mind and stop using for a while, just to show everyone I had it under control. But I was in denial. I didn't really want to change at all. I didn't see a reason to, because I hadn't really hit bottom. I hadn't lost enough yet. I didn't know it then, but the bottom wasn't far off.

In October, after the first exhibition game of the 1984-85 season, I left the San Antonio Spurs to play for the Houston Rockets. The night of the trade, the Spurs were playing the Rockets at the arena in San Antonio. I came to the game early, cleaned out my locker in the Spurs dressing room, walked across the gym to Houston's locker room, and put on a Houston uniform. That night, the Spurs whipped the

Rockets, beating us by twenty-five points. After the game in the locker room, I said to my new teammates, "Hey, guys. You remember this whipping, because we're going to get these guys next time we see them." They all looked at me like I was crazy. Hell, I'd been with the team no more than a few hours and I was talking like I'd been there for years, like I was their captain or something.

I did it because I was excited to be back with the Rockets. Houston felt like home to me because that's where I started my career in 1976 as the number-one draft pick in the NBA. Sometimes trades can really devastate a player, but this was a great trade for me. I now had a chance to play on a team that had a ton of talent, that wanted and needed me, and that had a very good chance to take the NBA title.

For me personally, things were very, very good, too. I wasn't using any drugs. Nothing. I swore to myself that I would stay clean. I had some incentive for that. Houston's coach then was Bill Fitch, and he put down the rule to me when they took me. He told me right up front, "If you ever have any problems, if we find you're using, I'm going to kick your butt off this club." Looking back, I credit Fitch for saving my life, but at the time I really thought he was a jerk.

Things went okay until that December, when we had a game scheduled in Portland with the Trailblazers. I missed the team flight because I'd been high on cocaine the night before and I was too paranoid to get on the plane with everybody. I called and made a reservation for the next flight to get to Portland. I got there and headed straight for the arena. The first thing Fitch said when he saw me is that I had to take a drug test right away. I did, and of course the test came back positive. And Fitch released me. Bang. Right then and there, I'm fired.

So I'm back in the same scenario — out of basketball again. I called my wife, Debbie, and said, "Hey, I been released. I'm on my way back. Please, can you pick me up at the airport?" I got on a plane and went back home to Houston. I thought it was over for me in basketball.

Debbie Lucas

This wasn't the first time John had been released. But when he called me to come pick him up this time, I think he felt that I'd maybe had enough and that I wasn't going to come get him. He sounded like a child who had run away from home and didn't know whether or not his parents were going to come get him. I could hear it in his voice. It was like he was saying, "My flight is coming in. Are you sure you're going to come get me?" And when I got to the airport to pick him up, it was like he was searching, looking this way and that with his eyes, like I wasn't going to be there or I wasn't going to show up. He looked like a sad, lost little puppy. I think he was worried that maybe this time he had really lost me and the kids.

After getting fired from the Rockets, I went back to treatment, this time in a clinic in Van Nuys, California. It was there that I had what I call my first awakening — what I would say today were my first feelings of surrender. For the first time in my life, I began to admit that I had a problem. I had been on a championship-caliber team with great players and a coach who was trying to help me. Suddenly, the situation had changed. I had no team to go back to and nothing to hope for. I was out of basketball. I had nothing — no hope. This time, I swore, things would be different. I was going to get well.

I got out of treatment in February 1985. I didn't even go home first to see my family. I went straight from the airport to talk with Bill Fitch. I told him, "I want my job back." And Bill said, "Okay, John, we're going to help you." So first Bill let me just be with the team, hanging around. Then I began to practice — but not with the team. After the guys had finished, I would have to work out with Bill. He wouldn't let me hang with or be like the rest of the guys. Then on the plane, we had what we called the hot seat. It was the seat next to Bill, and the guy who sat there had talk basketball the whole flight. The hot seat was my permanent seat!

That wasn't the end of it. After every game, I would have to go up to his room and watch the game videos with him. He'd keep me in his room until the middle of the night — 2:00 or 2:30 A.M. — and then he would say stuff like, "Okay, John, I guess it's safe for you to go to bed now. " He was trying to limit the time I would have by myself, to keep me from messing up. He never cut me any slack. I didn't like being treated like that at the time, but it was good for me. And Fitch was helping me in another way, too, because I learned a lot about basketball from him. I'd always played the game on instinct, and now I was seeing basketball from a different perspective. I was becoming a student of the game for the first time.

I was also trying to do something for my recovery, and so I went to Twelve Step meetings. Debbie and the kids and I would go together, and they would sit outside and wait for me. We were all doing well. Then, with twenty-eight games to go in the season, Fitch put me back on the team. What really amazed me was that in spite of all my trouble and my reputation as a user, the city of Houston was really behind me about getting back. I had a lot of support.

I finished out the regular season and I had a pretty good year, especially given all that I had been through. The Rockets got into the playoffs, but we ended up losing to Utah.

That summer I was feeling good. I wanted to do well in the upcoming season, so I worked out probably harder than I had in years. But I had a lot of idle time. I began to use a little bit again, and began to drink a little bit. I never felt I was doing anything wrong. I didn't see it as a relapse. The trouble was, I still didn't really accept that I had this disease. I had done the treatment and did some things after, like going to meetings, but I didn't have any aftercare. The NBA didn't have counselors and psychiatrists in every city like we have now, no network set up to provide help and support for guys who are trying to stay clean. But I kept working out, and pretty soon we were back in camp.

The 1985-86 season began, and there I was again with the Rockets. Everything seemed fine, and we are playing good ball. But I was backsliding — and I didn't see it. I was drinking occasionally and not going to any meetings. I wasn't doing anything whatsoever for my recovery — nothing that I was supposed to do. And so things just kept getting worse.

Debbie Lucas

I had thought after John went to Van Nuys that maybe he had finally gotten through all of this. He got off to a good start, going to his meetings and all. He was clean for a quite a while, but I just had a feeling that he wasn't through with it yet.

Then one day I realized that John had been saying that he was having colds all the time, and he had started taking Nyquil. Of course that has alcohol in it, and he was practically taking it by the case. Nobody needs that much Nyquil just for a cold. Then he started drinking, and I suspected he was doing cocaine again, too. I would be sleeping, and then I would wake up and he would just be standing over me, looking.

Coke users are very paranoid. He would accuse me of having a boyfriend, or say things like, "Where were you when I called?" I could have been out in the yard with the kids or at the store, but he was thinking that I was out running around or I don't know what. Or he would want to know who was at the house, thinking that someone must have been there and that's why I didn't answer the phone. If you have ever lived with a coke addict, you can tell they are using, and I knew John was on that road again. It was terrible. I was at the point where I didn't know what to do anymore. I know now I did some things that really didn't help, that were pretty dumb, but I didn't know what else to do. I'd never been in that kind of situation before - none of us had. And he would beg me not to turn him in, not to ruin his career. Of course, he was ruining it himself anyway, but he couldn't see that.

For a long time, I tried to stop him from going out at night and using. When he came home in that condition, as soon as he hit the house I'd lock the door. We had deadbolt locks that had to be locked with a key from the inside, so I would lock the door and hide the key. As I look back, it was really pretty silly. He could have gone out of a window anytime, but for some reason, he never thought about it. I'd hide the key somewhere before I went to bed. Then I would wake up at night, feeling him searching up under my pillow or just standing over me, staring.

Other times, when he'd go out, the kids and I would try to follow him in the car, or we would ride with him when he was intoxicated, thinking it would somehow keep him from going places. It didn't. He would even pick up his drugs while we sat in the car. And the kids, Tarvia and John, Jr., were really little at the time. They didn't know. For them, it was just another ride in the car with Daddy, like he had bought some potato chips and they were just eating and riding.

It took me a while to see that this wasn't doing anybody any good. One night when I tried to keep him home was one of the final straws. I knew he wanted to be going out, but he came in and got into bed as if he wasn't going anywhere. Then, next thing I knew, I heard the door and he was out. I got the kids and got in the other car and I followed him. He knew I was following him. He would run red lights to lose me, but I kept behind him. Really, I don't know what I was thinking I would do, but I kept following. Finally, we got to a corner and the light was green. John stopped and waited until the light turned red. Then he took off. Well, I wasn't going to go and kill my kids trying to follow him. That's when I said to myself, "That's it, I'm fed up, and I just can't help him anymore."

I took the kids back home and got them to bed. But I couldn't sleep at all. I was completely flipped out. I was up all night, looking out the window and hoping he would come home, watching every car that passed by, hoping and praying the police didn't pick him up and that I wouldn't have to go downtown and pick him up at jail — or worse, at the hospital.

God, it was so stressful and I cried a lot. And by now it was bad, not just for me and the kids, but for his family, too. He had us playing against each other: He was telling his family that I was the problem, and then he was telling me that his family was the problem. We couldn't help each other either because we didn't really understand what was going on. And they still didn't really know just how bad things were. But that summer when he was back home in Durham visiting his parents, his addiction was so bad that he didn't care that they knew he was using. He would stay out late all the time, or not come home for a day or two or three at a time.

The 1985-86 season wasn't going too badly, and while I did miss some practices, I made all the games. Whenever I missed practice, Fitch would make me take a drug test. But I got around that by using other people's urine for my sample. I'd just make the switch when I was supposed to get the sample. They suspected I was using, but the tests kept coming up negative. They couldn't do anything because they had no proof. I thought I was just too clever — until that March.

On March 14, we played the Boston Celtics in a closely contested game. One of the Celtics had a breakaway shot and there was a foul. I got really upset over the play and got a technical. Fitch got pretty angry at me and yanked me out of the game for getting the "T." After the game, I was still upset about the call, and even more angry at Fitch for pulling me from the game, which we lost in the final seconds.

The team was having a postgame promotional party that I went to, and before I left, I talked a friend of mine into leaving a gram of cocaine in my car for me. Debbie and I got home, and as usual she locked the deadbolt. She knew I was still using and always wanting to go out. That night in particular, I really couldn't sit still. I wanted out bad. While she was getting ready for bed, I noticed that she had left the keys in the door. I grabbed them and ran out the door, locking them in the house.

Debbie Lucas

We were home and John had already taken off his shoes. I went to do something with the kids. Next thing I know, I hear the door and he's left the house fully dressed in a suit and tie — but in his stocking feet. That's how bad he wanted to get out. I couldn't go run after him, and after a few hours went by, my cousin who was visiting me went out looking for John. He found John somewhere, and my cousin said it was like some movie chase scene trying to catch up with John. But John gave him the slip, and he was gone for the night.

The next morning — this was March 15 — I came to from what you'd have to call a blackout. I was coming off a binge in downtown Houston at 7:00 A.M. I'm looking for my car, but I can't even remember if I had driven it. I'm trying not to be recognized, but here I am, with shades on, filthy, in my suit, urine all over my pants, no shoes, five pairs of socks on my feet, and I don't remember nothing about the night before. And, of course, I missed the 9:30 A.M. practice that day.

The next day I went over to the arena as usual for our morning practice. We were scheduled against Portland that night. After the shoot-around, Fitch said, "Let's go, it's time for your test." But this time it was different. Fitch crossed me up. He went in the locker room and stood right next to me so I couldn't use anyone else's urine for the test. Late that afternoon, I came back to the arena to dress for the game, and the results were back: positive. I was sitting in the locker room, and Bill says, "You're doing drugs. Go put your street clothes back on and sit on the bench for the game."

Now this was major news, so before the game there were reporters everywhere and I was telling the media and everybody that the test was negative. I thought that it was going to be all right. I knew it was positive, but I thought management would just take care of it privately. I didn't think they'd go public or release me. I sat on the bench and everyone was taking pictures of me. I was the whole focus of the game. It was unbelievable. And here I was sitting there telling the biggest lie of my life in front of 15,500 people. Later that night, when the game came on, Bill put off the media and said the results weren't in.

Tom Nissalke, former NBA coach and longtime Lucas friend
I had come down to Houston for that game and to visit the

president of the team, who was a good friend of mine. Of course I stopped to see John. We had become very good friends during the first two years of his pro career when he played for me in Houston. We had kept in close touch through the years.

That day, at the hotel next to the arena, the Houston general manager came over to me in the lobby and said, "Your guy" — he always referred to John as "your guy" — "he didn't show up for practice today, and we're going to have to test him." That night, when I saw John wasn't dressed for the game, I went up to him and asked how he was doing. He said, "Oh, hey, I'm okay. No problem, no problem." Then the next day it comes out. Drugs again.

That's when it really hit home for me that John was really in trouble. Over the years we had always been able to talk freely and honestly with one another — or so I thought. I'd heard rumors about his drug use, of course, and I'd talked to him more than once about it. I knew he did a little something now and then, at least that's what he'd said. And now he had lied to me. I realized at that moment that if he could lie to me — his first coach and very close friend — he could lie to anyone. I knew this drug thing was out of control for him.

After the game, Fitch told me the team would call me the next morning at home to let me know if I should come to practice. So I'm sitting there watching the clock, and pretty soon it's 9:30...10:00...10:30...and no call from the team. So I called them, and they said they hadn't made a decision yet. Then, about two minutes after I hung up, they called back and told me they were going to release me.

I was dead inside. I couldn't move or hardly talk. I sat at home most of the day. Late in the afternoon, a friend and counselor, Len Goth, came over to help me. Debbie was there, too, and they were talking to me about going into treatment. I realized that I didn't have another chance. By not letting anyone talk him out of kicking me off the team,

Bill Fitch probably saved my life. I always thought I would get one more chance. I thought somebody was going to help, that a parachute would be there somehow.

I said, "Yes. Yes, I'll go to Van Nuys again," and this time I meant it. This time something had happened. That night out on my binge, I think I was trying to get caught. I was too afraid to turn myself in, but I was sick and tired of living the way I was. I had finally hit rock bottom. I had lost my job — again. I'd been out all night God only knows where in Houston, I'd come to with urine all over my clothes, filthy, my socks looking like I'd run through mud puddles, wearing shades, and trying not to be John Lucas. I had gotten into so much pain this time, I didn't care if I never played basketball again, I didn't care. I just wanted drugs out of my life. I just wanted to be free.

CHAPTER 2

EARLY CHILDHOOD

I had a pretty typical life as a young black kid living in the South just as segregation was beginning to break up. I was born in Oxford, North Carolina, but when I was pretty young, my family — my parents, John, Sr., and Blondola; my sister, Cheryl, who is six years older than me; and I — moved to the house where we did most of our growing up, in what was to us a big city — Durham. Duke University was there, the University of North Carolina was six miles up the road, and North Carolina State was only twenty-five miles away. My father was a high school principal, and he took a job at what was probably the biggest black high school in the state, Hillside High.

Blondola Lucas

From the time John was very young, he's been charismatic and very loving. I never dreaded his middle-of-the-night feedings, because when he woke up, he wouldn't be crying. He'd be smiling and just pulling me in to feed him, and I was going to enjoy doing it.

He could always get almost anything he wanted from me, his dad, and his sister. He was just a little darling. I don't know exactly how to describe this — he wasn't what you'd

*call a "kissy- kissy" child, but people just seemed to like him.
He was the kind you always wanted to pinch or kiss or hug.*

*When you look at John's hands today, you'll see how
large they are. He's always had those big hands, and he
could use them to take your face and just almost control you
with his movements. He's always been strong-willed, but not
overbearing, because you always felt his love, too.*

My elementary school — C. C. Spaulding — was only one block from
my father's school. After classes let out at about 2:30 P.M., I'd go to
Hillside instead of going straight home. I'd go up to my father's office
to do my homework. Hanging at the high school gave me a chance to
be with my dad and ride home from school with him. The other reason
I didn't want to go right home after school was because my mom wasn't
home either. She was the assistant principal at Durham's Shepard Junior
High. So my dad and I would generally go on home together. I also
knew that waiting for him would sometimes mean a little ride around
town in the car if he had to stop by the post office or do some other
errand after work. I loved to do that with him, especially if I could go
home and tell my sister I'd got a ride and she hadn't.

The real attraction of Hillside for me, though, was tennis, basketball, and baseball — sports, in other words. After I did my homework,
I'd go to the gym to watch the high school guys practice and play. Already
by the time I was about ten years old, I was very fond of athletics.

It was at Hillside that I also met a great guy, the late Carl Easterling.
Besides my father and mother, Coach Easterling, who was the high
school tennis and basketball coach, was my most important role model
during my grade school and high school years.

My parents, Cheryl, and I did a lot together. We were a very close
family. Because of my parents' involvement in education, we traveled to
many, many activities as a family unit — whether it was going to a PTA
meeting or an NEA [National Education Association] convention — as
well as going to the beach, visiting relatives, and so forth. My parents
say neither Cheryl nor I really caused them much trouble. They were

strict with us when it came to discipline. Durham was a smaller city then, one that had a pretty tight community. It wouldn't have done us any good to step out of line, because there were people my parents knew all over town. If I did something wrong, my parents would hear about it from someone — and pretty quickly. And with both my parents in education, well, it was hard to be out of their reach, especially during the school year. We were a religious family and went together to church each Sunday. Cheryl and I had to go to Sunday school, too. My parents were — and still are — very loving. They gave us a lot of attention — and punishment if we needed it. This time together with my family continued pretty much until I started playing tennis so much in the summers.

John Lucas, Sr.

John's strength of will and boldness started to show very early. We had a pretty structured life at home, and sometimes John would question me. He'd say, "Why do we always have to do what you want to do? Why can't I make a suggestion?" So we'd have a little talk about it. As the children grew older, we gave them more say in our decisions. I'd say something like, "This would be a good evening to go over and see your grandmother. Would you like to go?" We weren't exactly like every other family then, especially with both Blond and I working full time. And life just wasn't as fast then as it is today. Even though we both worked, Blond and I still had a lot of time with the children, and we made a point of taking them with us on trips.

I was pretty conscientious about my studies. If I wasn't, my teachers would mention it to my parents, who were strict about my studies and homework. They regulated my time carefully to make sure I put enough effort into my studies. I really saw my schoolwork as a necessity, though, as something I *had* to do. I was smart enough and worked hard enough to do okay in school, and I was in the upper quarter of my class. But I knew I wasn't the best. My heart just wasn't in my studies — it was in sports. Basketball and tennis came especially easy to me. I loved those games, and I played whenever I could.

I was never particularly book smart, but I was really innovative and creative. I would rather invent a new way of doing something than just follow the way everyone else did it. I liked that kind of challenge. If I came up with an idea and was allowed to carry through on it, I would stick with it.

The institutional way of studying and learning just wasn't interesting or exciting. Take studying history. You had to sit there and memorize a lot of names and dates and battles and wars. I thought, "So what?" To my way of thinking, the schoolbook already had everything mapped out for me, and that left me with no interest in studies. School wasn't exciting or challenging to me.

And what I really loved was a challenge. If I could figure out on my own how to do something, that was more of a challenge, and I would always do it. That's what appealed to me so much about sports. One reason I loved tennis, for instance, was that I never knew how the next point was going to be played. Every opponent was different, and each played the game a little differently. The same for basketball. You had ten guys on the floor, and you couldn't control what everyone was going to do. It wasn't all laid out for you. You had to think all the time and be innovative. I didn't know how I was going to play the next game or match, but I always knew what was next in school.

While schoolwork was monotonous, it was something I was able to get done. I was smart enough that I didn't have to work so hard at it, and I just kind of tried to get through it. I certainly didn't put my heart and soul into it like I was starting to do in sports.

Now I can see that I was developing a liking for living a little off the beaten path. The clothes I liked as a little kid were a little bit different, a little bit flashier, a little bit more trendy than what most kids wore.

John Lucas, Sr.

John was competitive from a very young age. When he was very little, we would play with balls on the floor— rolling them back and forth to each other. When he accomplished things, you would see a broad smile on his face. I think for him it was a matter of accomplishment, of being able to do something himself. He was always highly motivated and a self-starter, too. He would come to us or his sister and want us to play with him. Even this young, he'd be very disappointed if he sensed that someone was allowing him an advantage. He wanted to win and to make the achievement on his own without anyone providing some advantage for him. He showed independence and put forth a lot of energy when there was something he wanted to accomplish.

My sister Cheryl likes to say that I began my basketball career playing with her when I was eight or nine years old. She and I would use aluminum foil balls and throw them into trash baskets around the house. You can imagine what this was like, us running around the house, guarding each other, going from room to room shooting at wastebaskets.

About this same time, I started going with my family to watch tennis tournaments in the area. Tennis was popular at the time, and my parents liked to watch the good players. My dad, in fact, played pretty well himself. Then, in fifth grade, I started hanging out with the high school tennis team. I helped the players after school at their practices while I was waiting for my father to finish work. I would chase down balls for them because there were no backstops for the courts then. They were really glad for the help, because it saved them a lot of extra running around. After a bit, I came up with the idea to take someone's racket, stop the balls with it, and knock them back to the players. That's what began my interest in playing tennis.

By this time I'd gotten to know Coach Easterling pretty well from being around the school. I'd always try to shoot baskets with the older guys, and I was trying to play tennis, too. Easterling saw my interest and my ability, I guess, and he quickly became both my basketball and tennis coach on an informal basis. After that, I would be in the gym at 2:30 P.M. *every* day. When summer came around, he would teach me tennis.

Tennis and basketball weren't the only sports I was involved in then. I loved to play just about any sport when I was a child — badminton, baseball, football, whatever — and I was willing to play with just about anyone, as long as they would give me a good game.

Blondola Lucas

John was always confident, and he always wanted to play with the best. A neighbor of ours, Mr. Boyd, often played badminton with John, and his wife just loved John to death. Anytime Mr. Boyd wouldn't want to go out and play, John would go to his wife and say, "Would you ask Mr. Boyd to come out and play with me?" and she would send him right out.

On this particular day, Mr. Boyd didn't really want to play, but he went out just to accommodate John. They played a quick game, and John won.

Mr. Boyd went on back in the house, and a few minutes later, John came home. He said to me, "Mother, guess what? Mr. Boyd didn't really play me today because he let me win. I'm going to tell Mrs. Boyd." I said, "Well that's up to you, John. I wasn't in the game, so you do whatever you have to do."

So John went over there and got Mrs. Boyd to come to the door. He said, "Mrs. Boyd, Mr. Boyd let me win and I don't think that's right, so make him come and play again." So she sent Mr. Boyd back out, and this time John really had to work for his win. Afterwards, John went back to Mrs. Boyd, and said, "Well, I got my game. Thanks a lot," and then he came on home. Lucas [John, Sr.] and I still laugh about that.

I remember how John was always trying to get Lucas to

play tennis with him, and Lucas would always say, "Oh, you don't want to play me." This one time, though, Lucas agreed to play John, and when they got ready to go, I was in the kitchen. When they went by the kitchen window, John called in to me, "Momma, I'm taking Daddy out to the tennis court," and Lucas whispered, "I'm going to eat him up. The little fellow will be back in a few minutes."

So they left, and they stayed and stayed, and when they came back, I knew Lucas had beat John - John wasn't saying anything. He was quiet. So I said to him, "Oh, your daddy put a whipping on you, didn't he!" And he said, "Guess what, Momma! Daddy beat me." I said, "No, did he?" John said, "Yeah, he beat me good." But after John left the room, Lucas said, "I didn't really beat him, I just outsmarted him!"

My father had played and coached tennis when he was young. That time he beat me, well, it blew my mind. But it was very important to me, because in my mind, my father was outside the realm of the beatable. I'd already been pretty successful in tennis by this time; I'd taken some older guys. Getting beaten by my father just two games with me playing my best was enough for me to still think he was like God. As a young kid, I watched his every move, and though my mother ran the household and I loved her very much, in reality, my father was the role model that I watched.

In 1965, the summer I was in sixth grade, I started to go over to the Fayetteville Street fire station just down the street from our house. The firemen had a Ping-Pong table there in their recreation room, and since they needed something to do with their time, they played a lot. So I would go over and play with them, and it wasn't long before I started getting pretty good. They worked with me, and after not so many months, they sponsored me for regional and state championships. Well, I won the North Carolina state championship. It was sort of phenomenal because not only was I pretty young, but I was still very short.

I was always into competition and I only wanted to play with the best. I was confident and always felt I could win. But there was one person I never did beat: my grandmother. I loved her a lot, and went to visit her whenever I could. Every time I saw her, the day was spent playing checkers. We would take time for lunch and dinner, but that was all. I never did beat her, and she lived to be ninety-three. Actually, my father played her a number of times, too, and couldn't beat her either. She was *damn* good!

I think a lot of people believe that my parents pushed me to practice and play, but they *never* had to tell me to practice. If anything, they had the opposite problem. They'd have to come get me sometimes at school because I had stayed too long. That would really embarrass me; when they got there, my father would say, "What are you doing here?" He'd tell me I'd been out too long. "Either learn to come home at the time you're supposed to come, or no more practice," he'd say. I can still hear my father's voice today. But never once did my parents ever tell me to go practice tennis or basketball. I loved practice. The whole time I was in high school, I hit a thousand balls every morning against the back of the Hillside school gym, out there by myself working on my serve or whatever.

Summers during grade school meant playing tennis and attending basketball and tennis camps. During the school year, it was the same: playing in the gym after school during the week, and then tournaments and camps on weekends. I would get in a little baseball sometimes, but not often. Tennis and basketball were pretty much what I did.

Spending so much time in sports also meant spending a fair amount of time away from my parents. Coach Easterling became a sort of second father for me, which was okay with my parents. They felt that if Coach Easterling was with me, it would be as if my dad was there. And I knew that my dad regarded him and the other coaches I'd be with as important authority figures. They had my parents' blessing to discipline me if necessary.

Lots of kids like to compete, certainly, but for me, competition was everything. One time in the fifth grade we were having a baseball game during school. It was the boys against the girls. The girls were cheating — at least we boys thought so — and I got so furious with my teacher because she wouldn't put a stop to it that she wouldn't allow me to play the next day. It was all about winning. For me this wasn't about *girls* winning. I couldn't have cared less. It was about winning, period. Everything I did was of a competitive nature.

Part of that drive to work hard came from seeing how hard my father worked. He would come home, eat dinner, and go back to his office at school to work some more. My father was a highly respected man in education, so I figured that if all his work was paying off with accolades for him, my work — which was sports — would pay off with accolades for me. There was nothing I liked better than playing in tournaments and winning. And I liked the focus that you needed to have to be successful in sports.

I also saw the way my father worked with people. He was a people person and a great organizer. He knew how to get people together to do things, so I loved to take the organizer role, too, even as a young kid.

Had I been born even ten years earlier, things might have been very different for me. But at this time, opportunities for sports participation and competition were growing as part of the social changes taking place in society. Desegregation was making some difference, and this was also the beginning of a growing interest in organized recreation. Recreational programs were being started and more tennis courts and gymnasiums were being built. There were growing opportunities for kids like me not only to start early in a sport and stay with it, but to find levels of competition that would develop your potential.

John Lucas, Sr.

At this time, John was able to find a lot of acceptance in the group sports he was involved in, especially in basketball. He was achieving well and beginning to be selected for all-conference teams. Tennis was not yet accessible to all persons in the community because of racial prejudice, and John did meet with discrimination. Sometimes, of course, they would accommodate John because of his skill, but often he was really alone in the tennis camps. He was ignored because of his race, and sometimes not included in the general activities with the rest of the boys. I think that might have caused him to think that a team sport would be better for him, even though he was performing very well in tennis.

At this age, of course, I was too young to be working at a job, so I did sports. There was nothing I liked better than to work hard and win at any kind of athletic competion. Though I didn't realize it for many years, I was actually depriving myself of my childhood. From third grade on, I never really spent a summer like most kids do. I never climbed trees or went fishing. To this day, I still don't know how to swim. I've never played street ball or hockey, and I don't even ride a bike.

In school, I had my friends like any kids do. But I never spent much time with any of them outside of school — like walking home from school together, flying kites, reading comics, or just hanging out — because I would always have a game to go to, or my coach might need to talk to my team. By the time the game was done, there'd be nobody to walk with. When I'd get home, I'd have to eat dinner and do my homework, and then it was time to go to bed. I just didn't have any free time that wasn't involved with sports.

I spent some time with the children of the families that my family mingled with — relatives or people from the church we went to. These were more like brother-sister relationships than friendships, since I really grew up with these kids. I also had certain buddies I'd invite along when my family was going someplace fun. And it seemed like we were always going to someone's birthday party.

I think my dad would have liked me to be a Boy Scout. I joined for a while, but I didn't like the activities, like the Christmas parade they did every year. At church on Sunday, they would sometimes honor the Eagle Scouts, and the guys I hung around with thought the scouts were a bunch of stiffs. We thought that if you didn't play sports, you were just a nerd. And besides, I couldn't keep up with my uniform — I kept losing my scarf! Probably the biggest factor, though, was that the troops had their meetings on Saturday mornings, and that's when I'd be over at the gym or the community recreation center playing in pickup games with the older guys.

Most of the time I hung with friends from the teams I played on. I never had a lot of friends — I had *teammates*. We'd play sports, and then we would go to someone's house. My mom would always fix some food for us for lunch or give us snacks after school. Mom says she never makes homemade lemonade anymore because she made so much of it for us when I was a kid!

I just didn't feel I had much in common with people who weren't athletes. Nobody was making me do this; I liked hanging with kids who were exceptionally talented at what they were doing. I loved doing sports, and I didn't feel deprived or lonely. It was only much later that I could see what was happening to me, what I was giving up and missing because of this single-minded focus on sports.

As I think about this today, I ask myself if maybe I haven't been addicted — or had addictive behaviors — ever since I was a young kid. I didn't have one or two baseball cards, I had to have them all or I didn't want any. I didn't want to play in one or two of the tennis tournaments for the summer, I wanted to play *all* of them.

I never saw any alcohol or other drugs at my house. My parents didn't drink at home that I remember, although I do recall one time when I was maybe ten or eleven years old when Cheryl and I went to Philadelphia with my parents to visit some friends of theirs. The adults were all drinking champagne. I remember telling them that I wanted some champagne, too, so they gave me a champagne glass filled with 7-Up. A little while later, I told my mother that I had to go right to sleep because I thought I was drunk!

I loved my parents very much, but even at this age, I was spending less and less time with them. Most of our time together was either in a student-teacher relationship or athlete-parent relationship. When we were together as a family, we had a great time and we were very close — it's just that those times were coming less and less often, especially as I got more involved with sports. My activities, together with their work load, meant that summers were the only time we could all be home together. But even then, we all had things to do. Maybe we'd go to an NEA convention together, go to the beach for a vacation, or visit some relatives. But once I got into junior high school, I spent most of the summer with Coach Easterling playing tennis.

From the time I was about ten years old until I was well into my addiction, I really didn't see the love and concern that was there from my parents. I knew I was loved and all, but we never had to go through anything, any crisis, that would really test the substance or strength of our love. It was all gift-wrapped. It seemed to me that I went from having unconditional love for my parents early in my life to what I call straight "respect" love. You're my father, my mother, and I respect you, so I love you.

I practically worshipped my father, and he played a very big role in my life at that time. My mother took great care of me — made sure I was clean and that I had the right clothes, helped me with my homework. I don't remember feeling a great need for my mother earlier in life, but I needed her — and she was there for me — when I finally began to become an adult. This didn't really happen until I faced my addiction. Only then did I again experience our love as total and unconditional.

CHAPTER 3

JUNIOR AND SENIOR HIGH SCHOOL

My new relationship with Coach Easterling really marked the beginning of my sports career. The more I hung around at Hillside High and the more I got into sports, the better Coach Easterling and I got to know each other. He took an interest in me as an athlete. When I started playing tennis, Easterling encouraged me to play more. He told me I had talent. I guess I was too young to understand what that really meant, but I decided to go along with him because I did like the game. I liked Easterling as a person, too. He'd also been coaching me informally in the winter in basketball. He was a kind man and a very good coach in both sports. Over the coming years, we would become very close. Looking back now, I don't think I would ever have gotten into tennis if Easterling hadn't encouraged me.

At the age of ten, just three months after I started working with Easterling on tennis, I began playing tennis both in Durham and around the southern part of North Carolina. He helped get me entered in an actual tournament in the summer of 1964, and I won. After that I believed what he was saying, and I decided to keep playing tennis. I found myself winning more matches, and that made me want to play even more. I wanted to play in tournaments, I wanted to play the best. I thought I would never, ever lose a tennis match.

John Lucas, Sr.

John really began to grow physically after he began playing tennis in his early teens. Maybe playing tennis stretched him out! He was playing basketball then, too, and he was also dabbling in football and baseball. John liked football. He had a great arm, and with his height and leadership skills, he would have make a great quarterback. But the Hillside coaches got together and decided that there was too much of a chance for John to be injured playing football, so they encouraged him to stay put in tennis and basketball. John didn't have the time or energy for another sport anyway. He could have been an excellent baseball player, too, but again, there just wasn't time. Tennis and basketball took up most of the year for him.

Along with Coach Easterling, my teammates and I spent spring and summer riding the tennis bus around southern North Carolina playing in kids' tennis tournaments. My family, friends of my parents, and people in my neighborhood in Durham supported me. They would donate money for me to go on these trips. It was a lot of fun traveling around with a bunch of guys and getting out of Durham. It was also a great way for me to work on my game because it exposed me to more competition that I could get in Durham.

When I was fourteen — this was in 1968 — I played in a big tournament in Durham for the first time — the Durham City-County Tennis Championships. I signed up for every event I was eligible to play in: fourteen-and-under singles and doubles. sixteen-and-under singles and doubles, eighteen-and-under singles and doubles, men's singles, men's doubles. I won seven events in that tournament, including men's singles.

Here I was not just playing, but winning, against guys much older than me. I was even gaining some national recognition now. That year, my picture was in *Sports Illustrated*, in the "Faces in the Crowd" section, which often highlights up-and-coming young athletes.

People who have followed tennis over the years might remember a guy named Walter "Whirlwind" Johnson, an incredible player in his day. A well-to-do black physician, Dr. Johnson worked with the best young black tennis players in tennis, including Althea Gibson and Arthur Ashe. In the summer Johnson would take a group of kids to the major American Tennis Association tournaments. Each kid received what amounted to a scholarship. Johnson's group would find ways to raise enough money between your family and other folks for you to go. He talked to me, my parents, and Coach Easterling about having me travel with his group, and Easterling agreed. Everyone felt it would be great experience for me.

Once I started with Johnson, who became my coach, I told him I didn't want to play the kids anymore because it wasn't any challenge. I always won. I was rarely losing any games to guys even a few years older, let alone sets or matches. Johnson agreed, and moved me up so I was playing in men's events. He was trying to prepare me for the next level, the United States Lawn Tennis Association (USLTA), which was the major circuit for tennis. It wasn't long before I began winning the men's tournaments, too.

I loved the competition, even when I lost. I lost the North Carolina State men's title two years in a row, at age fouteen and fifteen. A guy in his late twenties beat me both years for the championship. That I was challenging someone that experienced was really exciting to me, that and the big crowds. Here I was playing in front of thirteen thousand people. I felt a lot older than my age.

After two summers with Dr. Johnson, my parents felt the program with him wasn't working out the way they wanted, and they decided to have me go back with Coach Easterling again. My parents had gotten a letter saying that I wasn't as neat as I needed to be, and they didn't like that. Players were supposed to do dishes and clean and whatever, which was something different for me because I didn't have regular chores at home. I didn't have to clean or rake leaves or wash dishes or make my bed because of my sports activities. I led a special life. So my father told them he didn't want me going to somebody else's house to be cleaning and washing dishes. He said, "What if John cuts his hand on a knife or some broken glass?"

So my parents weren't happy with Dr. Johnson, and I also decided that I didn't like going with him. I liked my teammates and the competition there, but I also liked the freedom of being on my own. I preferred traveling with my parents or with Coach Easterling, so the next year my parents just raised the money for me to travel with him, and that's what I did.

Coach Easterling was playing a bigger and bigger role in my life now — probably more of an influence than my father. I could share anything with him. Being at a predominately black school, everybody knew about everybody else, so it wasn't a big deal that I wasn't with my parents so much anyway. I had a lot of role models, men like Easterling and other coaches and teachers who my parents liked, respected, and trusted to look after me. Easterling very much shaped me both as a man and as an athlete. I have to give him a lot of the credit for who I was — and who I am today.

Given the level of competition I'd had during the summers traveling with Easterling and Johnson, high school tennis was not much of a challenge. I had been playing number one in singles and doubles since my first day on the team in tenth grade. By the end of my junior year, I had still never lost a set.

The director of the North Carolina High School Athletic Association (NCHSAA) always laughed at a couple little habits I had. Each player going to the state tournament had to bring two cans of balls, and the loser of each match would have to give the extra can to the winner. Well, I always brought only one can to the tournament. To bring more would be an admission that I might lose — which I never did. The other thing he use to kid me about was that I never took off my warm-ups for my matches. I was showing that I wasn't going to have to work hard enough in the match to need to change out of them.

Competition and winning were getting more and more important to me, and I'd gotten pretty intense. I had met Arthur Ashe a few times, and he had heard of my playing. Some people were already calling me the next Arthur Ashe. During high school, I saw Arthur play a match in North Carolina against some local guy, and this guy beat Ashe. Arthur was very stoic. He didn't show any emotion out on the court, and it didn't seem to bother him at all that he'd lost the match.

I thought that you could win all the time, and it *really* bothered me. I went up to him after the match and said to him, "What are you doing getting *beat*? This ain't *normal*!!" I figured, what's your problem? You're the best in the world, so what are you doing losing? I thought there was something wrong with him, and my friends and I really took it to heart. We told him we were really disappointed that he lost.

Now that I'm older, I understand the situation — what it takes to travel, to play all the time. It's tiring. So maybe Arthur was just beat, maybe he had an off day, maybe he was playing there just as a favor to Walter Johnson and didn't really care about winning. But at the time, the only thing I could see was that this guy was playing, and he's supposed to win. I *hated* losing. I couldn't understand why it didn't bother him that much.

The pattern of winning was everywhere in my life. Here I was, playing against men — and beating them. Now at this age, it seems to me that a person's goal ought to be to become an adult, not to beat adults. But as a teenager, I equated beating adults with *being* an adult. And if I was beating adults at age fifteen, where was the next level? At some point, there wouldn't be one — and when I came face to face with that reality a few years later, I'd be in trouble.

If it seems that as a teenager I still didn't have much of a life outside of sports, that's true. The pattern that began when I was in elementary school just got more definite in junior and senior high. When basketball season ended, tennis would start. The day after school got out, I would leave for summer tennis camps and tournaments. I wasn't home much until the week before school started, and soon after that, basketball season would start again. That was my year.

Most of my social life was spent with my teammates — the basketball team in the winter and the tennis guys in the summer. Outside of sports, I didn't have many close friends because I wasn't around. This life also kept me from seeing kids who had other interests besides sports, kids who had more balanced lives.

I was a still popular because of being in sports, and I always had people to hang with in school. I discovered that being good in sports meant it wasn't too much trouble to get dates and have friends. I did regular social things and went to some social events, but they weren't so important to me. I didn't go to the prom, I didn't do so much dancing and partying. I was a dedicated athlete. I was a little scared of girls, too, like most boys are in junior and senior high school. And besides, I'd felt nearly since we met in third grade, that Debbie Fozard was the only girl for me, the one I was going to marry.

Blond Lucas

John always said, "I really am going to marry Debbie." In high school, John liked a lot of girls. We talked one time about the number of girls he would date and so on, but he would say, "But Debbie's going to be my wife." He always talked about wanting to go out with other girls. He always liked Debbie, but he would never just settle down and court her. He would have two or three different girls he'd be seeing, but he was never too serious about them.

Debbie Lucas

John and I first met when we were eight years old. We grew up four blocks from each other, we were in the same class in sixth grade, and we went to junior and senior high together. His mom was my ninth grade English teacher and the dean of women at our junior high, and his dad was the principal of our high school.

John teased me a lot all through junior high and senior high. He'd be doing something silly or saying something silly, then he'd say something like, "I'm going to marry you, girl." But at the same time, he was popular with other girls. He was the seventh grader with a ninth-grade girlfriend, and the tenth grader with a twelfth-grade girlfriend. I think he just thought he was Mr. Popularity. When he'd be talking to me, I'd always say things like, "I wouldn't marry you if you were the last person on Earth," because I thought he was too full of himself.

Everybody did like John. He was just a happy guy. He was the type that always had a joke or something for you every day. He was the kid who, when he passed your classroom, would stop and do something silly outside the door. In our high school yearbook, people predicted that he was going to be a stand-up comedian on The Ed Sullivan Show.

John's always been like the kid in your hometown that everybody says is going to do this or that because of his ability in school. He was an incredibly talented athlete. Very few kids start as point guard for the varsity team in the tenth grade. And that was just basketball. His tennis was outstanding, too. Me, I always liked his tennis better than his basketball. He was a better tennis player than a basketball player as far as I'm concerned.

John didn't have any problems in junior and senior high. I think that was something that really helped me get through the tough times in our relationship — I knew him before his drug problem.

Even though I was very confident on the court or the floor and popular in school, I really didn't feel confident of myself in everyday social settings. I had fears and emotions that I never recognized in myself. I was a kid with pimples, so I didn't really think I was attractive. I was like any normal teenager — very self-conscious — and I never talked about this or other feelings. I was able to put on a good show, but inside I had a lot of fears.

Two things I really hated — and this was the reason I competed so hard in sports — were rejection and failure, or what I perceived to be failure. I never knew when good was good enough. I was never happy unless we won, unless I was the best player. I was scared to talk to girls, too, even though I could do it, and if a girl told me no for a date or something, I'd get really down on myself.

I felt different from other students, too — not because of my athletic ability, but because of who my parents were. Imagine being a teenager and your mom is the assistant principal and dean of discipline in your junior high and your dad is the principal of your high school. I didn't want this kind of notoriety. I just wanted to be one of the guys. Of course, the reality of it was that I *wasn't* different, that it didn't matter what my parents did — but I couldn't understand that at the time.

Because I was always playing sports with older guys, pretty much everybody I'd been around was a little older. I would hear in school on Mondays about the weekend goings-on at the Chicken Box. The Box was a kind of drive-in where everyone would go after basketball games, buy some fried chicken, and park in their cars to eat. Of course some people would be drinking beer or wine, too.

Even in tenth grade, I knew virtually nothing about alcohol, let alone other drugs. It was never discussed at all in my home. The first time I drank, I was fifteen. I'd heard people talking about drinking beer or wine, but I still really didn't have any idea what to expect. I didn't even like the taste of it. The first beer I had tasted horrible. I had to get used to it.

After I'd drank a few times, I was surprised at alcohol's effect on me — it was powerful. I felt a part of the group, not separate. I seemed to lose my fears, that pressure I felt to be best, to succeed. I felt more confident with girls, too — like if a girl wouldn't go out with me or didn't like me, it didn't matter. I could say the things I always wanted say to her, and if I still got rejected, I could just put it off to being drunk. It was a way to handle rejection. And if she said yes to a date, I would tell myself that the beer helped me do my talking.

Alcohol gave me a sense of wholeness, a feeling very much like what I had on the basketball and tennis court. And it gave me a feeling of spirituality. I later found out that this was a false spirituality, an illusion. I would only find a true sense of spirituality much later in my recovery from addiction.

Even though I drank in high school, and in spite of the powerful feelings it created in me, I still never drank very much. It was more part of a social activity. It was never anything that I had to have, and besides,

I was too involved with sports to have time to hang with people at the Box very often.

I had been doing so well in tennis that when I got to my senior year, Coach Easterling encouraged me to go out for the U. S. Junior Davis Cup team. I was confident of my tennis, but I did have some doubts about making the team. Even Arthur Ashe hadn't played Junior Davis Cup tennis. But I agreed to give it a try.

When I was getting ready to go out to California for the Cup trials, I made a bet with my father. I really wanted a car — and not just any car. I wanted a little red Plymouth Barracuda. So I said to my dad, "If I make the Junior Davis Cup team, will you buy me that car?" And Dad said, "Yeah." I guess he thought it was a pretty safe bet!

Blond Lucas

John and I had vowed that we would not give either of the kids a car in high school. Cheryl had gotten through school without getting a car, so when John asked us to buy him a car if he made the team, we had to think on it a while. But we finally told John, "Okay, you make the team, we'll get you a car."

Once he got to California, John would call us at night and he would say, "There's no hope for me. I'm the only little black boy here. There's just no hope for me. They ain't going to give me a place on the team."

And I would say, "I didn't know you were like that. I didn't know they were playing the colors out there — black and white." And he said, "Momma, you know what I'm talking about." I said, "No, I don't. You go out and play and if you deserve it, you will win it."

He called every night saying that he didn't make the team. But I knew when he finally had, because when he called that time, he said, "What ya know, what ya know!" He was all up, so I said, "Did you make the team?" and he said, "What do you mean? Did I play?"

The night before he won, John called us and told Lucas, "I want you to go down to the Chrysler company and ask for Mr. Davis. Mr. Davis will tell you what kind of car I want. Now I don't have but one more night to make the team, and I want you to pick it up the minute I make the team."

After we hung up the phone with John, I said to Lucas, "Are you going down to the Chrysler company?" He said, "Yeah. I'm going to see if John knows what he's talking about to ask for Mr. Davis."

The next morning, we went down and met Mr. Davis. He showed us a red Barracuda that he was saving for John. You see, John had actually gone before he left and talked to Mr. Davis. He had picked out the one he wanted and told Mr. Davis, "This is the car that I want them to get for me."

Well, we felt we couldn't refuse to give John the car. So we talked with Cheryl about it because we wanted to be fair. She said, "Well, you promised and he made the team, so go ahead and give him a car. It won't bother me."

That's how he got his automobile. He was so confident he would make the team that he actually went down to pick the car he wanted beforehand!

I had played against some tough competition to make the Junior Davis Cup team. The other guys who made it included Jimmy Connors, Vitas Gerulaitis, Chico Hagey, George Hardy, Brian Teacher, and Sherwood Stewart — all of them pretty good tennis players.

I was so excited to get home and see my parents — and when I checked our garage, there was that bright red 'Cuda in the back! But now I had another problem. The car had a stick shift, and I didn't know how to drive one. I'd picked out a car I couldn't even drive! I had to get my mother and father to teach me how to shift it.

While I was in California trying to make the team, I had a couple experiences that I didn't pay much attention to at the time — but they did make an impression that I remembered later. Vitas Gerulaitis was one of my roommates. One evening, the day before the biggest game in tennis in my life, Vitas goes and stays out all night on Telegraph Avenue, and then comes back and wins his match. I'd been sitting there resting and just being a nervous wreck, and I remember saying to myself, "If it works for Vitas, it might work for me." Vitas wasn't doing drugs; it's just that he was out all night and still made the team. I couldn't believe someone could do that.

In California I saw a really different drug scene. People were using all kinds of stuff — marijuana, LSD, mescaline, you name it. It was nothing like that in Durham. Anyway, early in the week, I remember someone taking me to a halfway house to visit a friend of his who was there. I thought this was such a joke. I said to myself, "I'll *never* end up here. Something like that could *never* happen to me." Not that I was into drugs at the time, but already my ego was saying that nothing could beat me.

Later, when I started using, I thought drugs could never beat me, either. I got into a flat-out major competition with alcohol and drugs. One of the biggest problems I would have in recovering from my addiction was being unable to accept the idea of surrender — that I would have to concede defeat to drugs before I could get better. Surrender to win? We're talking crazy! That's talking nonsense! I was always taught that it's got to be 98 to 97, I win. In sports you always come up with another way to win, not a way to lose.

Making Davis Cup was really the culmination of a great high school tennis career. I was the first black to ever be named to the squad, and at age seventeen, the second youngest guy on the team. When I graduated, I was a two-time NCHSAA champion. In my high school years (grades 10 to 12), I had a string of 31 consecutive matches without a loss. During that time, I won 186 games and lost just 28, a feat unparalleled in the history of NCHSAA tennis. I was seeded first in the 1972 USLTA championships. Coach Easterling said I was the greatest natural athlete he'd ever seen. More than three hundred colleges and universities expressed an interest in me for tennis alone. I was, however, a two-sport All-American in high school.

My successes in basketball paralleled those in tennis, and they began early in my life, too. When I went to junior high school, I made the junior varsity team. It was obvious from the start, though, that I was too good to stay on that team. I got promoted right away, and I started for the junior high varsity all three years. My last year in junior high, the ninth grade, my team won fifteen games in a row and I lead the city in scoring. Going to high school meant leaving my mother, so to speak, since she was the assistant principal at my junior high school, and going to my father, who was principal of Hillside High.

John Lucas, Sr.

When John reached high school, there was a rule that players had to be on the junior varsity team before the varsity team. I was not in favor of changing the rule because I didn't want my child to be the one for whom an exception was made. I did, however, respond to the athletic community in the school. I left it up to both the coaches and the players to vote on the question. They agreed to let John play varsity, but at the time, there wasn't an opening on the team. John started out on the junior varsity team, but during the course of the year he got the elevation after one of the older boys was injured.

My father really didn't want me to be put on the varsity team because he felt people would see it as giving special treatment to his son. But Coach Easterling wasn't hearing any of that. Not only did I play varsity as a tenth grader, I started at guard. It seemed to me by now that anything I set my mind to achieve athletically I was able to do.

I loved basketball. I loved the challenge, especially at the guard position. You never knew what was going to happen, and the position called for both calculation and improvisation. You had to be thinking all the time. I considered myself more of a leader than a scorer in high school. I could score if I wanted to, certainly, or if I had to when everyone else went cold. I never worried about anyone stopping my scoring because no one could. In my senior year, I was the only player returning to the team. In our first game, everyone was pretty jittery, so I ended up taking a lot of shots. I got fifty-six points that day.

I really felt that a point guard who scores only eight or ten points a game is doing other things. He's leading the team. He has them under control. He keeps the big men happy. He's like a coach on the floor. Coach Easterling used to describe me as the general — a floor general.

I had some good years in high school. I led my conference in scoring every year, even though that wasn't my goal. I got an awful lot of assists, too. I averaged thirty-five points a game my senior year and led my team to the state tournament — that was something because there was very tough competition in North Carolina in those years.

In spite of my success in basketball, I think I would say that I have always been a better tennis player than basketball player. I didn't really need to practice so much for tennis, but I did for basketball. It just didn't come nearly as naturally to me and I had to work at it. I was good enough in both, though, to have contacts from 401 colleges and universities between the two sports.

Normally people are glad to get out of high school, but for me it was sad. One of the things I didn't like from the time I was a child was change. The bigger the change, the more difficult it was for me, so I really struggled at the end of high school. It was a time of sorrow. I was so comfortable there. I loved my teammates. What I really wanted was to take my whole basketball team with me to college. I wanted to take everybody with me everywhere I went. Not accepting change is a problem that stayed with me into my adult life.

By the time I finished high school, I had created some unrealistic goals for myself. I believed I could achieve anything I wanted to in sports. Also, I was obsessed with winning. I didn't have any other goals except to win. I never worried about being second; the thought that I might not win never even entered my head. I had been a sophomore starting varsity, and I was a teenager winning men's tennis titles.

Even with my athletic achievements, I had no sense that I was exceptional or had some special abilities. I thought nothing of what I was accomplishing. When I won a tournament, for instance, I would give my trophy to my parents. Each time I got one, I just wanted another one — I wanted to get all the trophies in the world. The one I'd just got didn't mean anything to me. I was never satisfied. Even when I was a young kid, I was running from myself to try to get to myself.

From this point in my life, I grew up only as an *athlete.* I wasn't getting the broad experiences I would need to be a balanced, mature adult. Instead, I took athletic principles and applied them to my daily living, even as a young kid. Nobody explicitly taught me these attitudes; they formed in my mind as a result of playing sports all the time.

Like many athletes, I believed that winning isn't everything, it's the only thing. I saw everything in terms of competition, even relationships. If I was competing with a guy to date the same girl, I had to win — I had to have her. I felt that the harder I worked, the luckier I'd get and the more I'd win. If I got into an argument with someone, I'd never back down. I'd get stronger and angrier. I wasn't going to lose any argument, because I was a winner.

Even with friends, a win was a win. There was no happy compromise. Either I win, or I lose. That's it. I didn't have the understanding that I developed later through my recovery that life can be a win-win situation, that there can be compromises. I had learned about life from sports, and in sports, someone *has* to win and someone *has* to lose. I had no idea how to turn the competition off. I was always *comparing* — my parents to your parents, my watch to your watch, my girl to yours.

If I met obstacles I couldn't do much about — like segregation — I'd try somehow to fight through them. Here was this young black kid playing in tournaments around the country where the players were predominately white — and at a time when integration was just beginning. I remember playing once in Chattanooga, Tennessee, and they called me for one foot fault after another during the match. There was no way I was faulting that much, but there was nothing I could do, and I ended up losing the match. At another match, I wasn't allowed to use the locker room or toilet facilities. I didn't let it bother me. I just kept playing tennis, going to tournaments, and winning.

On the occasions I wasn't playing so well, I'd get really frustrated really fast. I used to throw my racket all the time when I'd make mistakes. It wasn't very professional, of course, but I didn't think it was so bad. Then at one match, my father saw me do this, and afterwards, he told me, "If you throw your racquet, you won't ever play tennis again." From that incident I learned to never show emotion. I became a poker face. This became another sports principle that I carried into the rest of my life, and it had two effects. First, I decided to keep things inside and never show *any* emotion. Second, knowing that I enjoyed winning, I would try to avoid situations where I would need to get angry. Winning became a way to avoid feelings of frustration and anger. I would push hard to win so I wouldn't *need* to feel bad.

I developed these "sport/spiritual" life values even though I was raised with strong religious values and education. My parents were, and still are, really religious. As a young kid, I always said my prayers. I went to church every Sunday, too, but I had no earthly idea why I was there. Here again, the things that frustrated me about school — a lot of reading, everything already mapped out — came out with religion, too. Things that weren't a challenge to me just didn't much interest me.

As I got a little older and more perceptive, I saw a lot of people going to church and saying one thing, but they turned right around and did the opposite. Eventually it came to this: I would go to Sunday school, and then after it was over, we were supposed to go to church; instead, me and my friends would go to a place called Paul's Bar and Grill. I wasn't drinking or doing drugs, just hanging out with the other kids that didn't go either. While church was going on, we'd keep an eye out and then go back before it was over. We just hoped they didn't have a short sermon!

The only time I would have any religion was when I was about to lose a match. When I got in trouble — like one point from losing — I would say to myself, "If there's a God, make me win this match." I should have been saying at the beginning, "God, let me do the best I can." But no, I'd say, "If there's a God, make me win right now." That's how desperate I got about winning. And then when I didn't win, I'd say, "Well, there ain't no God. You didn't help me this time, so there can't be a God." I felt that if God didn't help me win, why should I bother with religion? I don't need this God. Actually, I was in competition to *be* God.

Years later, when I got into recovery and first heard the concept of believing in something greater than myself, I thought it was totally absurd. I thought *I* was the best. I had developed a belief system that was wrong.

All through elementary and secondary school, I had a tight structure around my life. I lived close to school, I was very close to my parents, and they were principals in my school. I had my coaches — especially Coach Easterling — who all knew me very well and were close to my parents. To really go astray wasn't possible at that time. When I went to college, that structure weakened some but remained strong.

A tight structure around me, involvement in sports to the exclusion of other activities, teammates as my only real friends, an overwhelming desire to compete and win, near total detachment from my emotions, the values of the sport life becoming my life values — these were like little streams flowing into the future. None of them individually were causing me much trouble now, but the potential for difficulty was always there.

CHAPTER 4

⬤

UNIVERSITY YEARS

With so many schools actively recruiting me, choosing the one to attend was not an easy decision. One factor, however, ruled out most of them and made me focus on the Atlantic Coast Conference (ACC) schools. During my senior year at Hillside, the ACC changed their eligibility rules to make it possible for freshmen to play varsity ball. In both junior and senior high school, I had played varsity as a freshman, and I was absolutely sure I could do it at the college level. I didn't want to waste my freshman year playing junior varsity.

I looked closely at a few schools, and the one that interested me most was the University of Maryland. My parents, Cheryl, and I all visited the campus and talked to the coach, Lefty Driesell. At the time I was a relative unknown in the area in spite of my popularity in and around Durham. Maryland was and is still a basketball hub with many great high school basketball programs, and at that time, there were a lot of great high school players.

I was also seriously considering UCLA, and they wanted me badly. UCLA was still a dynasty then under coach John Wooden. Wooden told me, however, that he wouldn't let me play both tennis and basketball, and I couldn't agree to that. I ultimately chose Maryland, primarily because of Driesell. I had talked to him a lot, and I really liked him as a person. Then, when I was close to making my decision, I asked him outright, "If I'm good enough to start, will you play me?" He said, "If you're the best player, son, you'll start." He was the only coach who told me that.

I had a set of more personal reasons for deciding on Maryland, too. While I wanted to get away from home, I still wanted to be close enough to get back to see my parents easily. As a college, Maryland would give me the same adrenaline rush *and* family environment that high school did — just on a little bigger scale. I would be only four hours from home, so people from home could get to me or to come to see my games. I wouldn't be out of sight. And what I hoped for came true. I remember one night, we were playing Duke at Maryland. Duke is located in Chapel Hill, just a few minutes from Durham, so a lot of Duke students knew about me. That night when we came out on the court, all these people in the stands started throwing tennis balls down at me. A big crowd had driven up for the game!

My parents would come up to the campus a lot, too, and my dad spent a lot of time running back and forth to watch me play. Cheryl would also visit, so we could really be together as a family there. Cheryl was living in Washington, D.C., only five or six miles from the campus. She and I were always very close, and I guess she became a kind of substitute for my mother. She was very protective of me — Cheryl and two good friends of hers, Vicky and John Roymer, really became my family there. Going to Maryland let me keep the same type of strong structure around me that I had in high school. And a final connection: Arthur Ashe's agent, a fellow named Donald Dell, had his office in Washington, too, so when I was being recruited by Maryland, Donald came over to see me.

I was really excited about playing college ball and about the possibility of playing as a freshman. I felt the pressure to do well, so I decided to attend summer school at Maryland. It was a way to get myself acclimated with the campus. I took a six-hour course load — not too much to take all my free time, but enough to let me see what classes would be like. Most importantly, I could play basketball with college guys. I was ready for everything when classes started in the fall.

When I came up to college, most people wanted and expected me to enter on a tennis scholarship, and I was eligible for a scholarship in both sports. I realized that even though I wanted to play both sports in college, I could only concentrate on one of them. At first, I didn't know how to decide what to do. I was projected to be the next Arthur Ashe, and that was a pretty strong force for me to play tennis. I talked to Arthur Ashe to get his ideas, and he wrote me a long letter with some suggestions about how to choose.

But the more I thought about it, the better basketball looked. I just didn't like the atmosphere that surrounded tennis. Because it wasn't a team sport, you traveled by yourself all the time. In spite of all the tennis I'd played, I never got to know any of the players because they were from all around the country. You'd go to some city to play against these good tennis players, and then as soon as the tournament was over, you left. It was a lonely life. There was no camaraderie among players in tennis like there was in basketball. I really liked the feeling of being on a team, so the way to go became clear — basketball — even though I was a better tennis player. I've always said that I was a born tennis player and a manufactured basketball player. I really worked to be good at basketball.

After all the practice I'd put in during the summer and early fall on my game, I felt I was ready for the basketball season to begin. I really wanted to be accepted and do well because I knew I was eligible as a freshman to play varsity basketball.

Lefty Driesell

John Lucas was simply a great athlete. He was the best damn basketball player you'd want to see right from day one. He came to us as a guy who'd broken Pete Maravich's high school scoring record. He was really too good. In his first two scrimmages as a freshman, he scored fifty points in the first game and forty the next. I had to tell him, "John, if you average all those points, you'll look great but we're not going to win many games that way. You've got to distribute the ball more, get it to other people, which he did. John was very

*coachable. He'd listen to you and do what you told him.
Some guys question you, but he didn't. He believed in what
you were doing and what you told him.*

This was 1972, a time when there was more experimentation with drugs on college campuses than ever before. As I've said, the only drug I ever saw in Durham was alcohol. Now I was on a campus where kids were trying all kinds of stuff. I was a little curious about all of this, but I still thought other drugs were really bad, and I had a healthy fear of them.

A few weeks before my first freshman game, though, some of my teammates and I were out for a good time — and someone had gotten hold of some LSD. I'll never forget this because it was the first time I tried a drug like this. Except I didn't really do it! I told them I took it, but I didn't. I was scared to death. They all took some and I drove the car. They couldn't believe I could drive the car and move around and do all the stuff I did, and so next time we did it — and I only did acid twice in my life — they watched me so I couldn't get away with not taking it.

Now this is the day before my first game. I'm a freshman and Lefty had told me I would not only be playing, but starting. I was really nervous. So what do I do the day before the biggest game of my life? I go take this acid. I freak out, and then I pass out. The next thing I know, my friend is smacking me, pow, pow. I'll never, ever forget that. I spent the rest of the night cowering on a sofa, pleading with them, saying, "Don't hit me. Don't hit me. What'd I do? Don't hit me. What'd I do?" We stayed out all night at some guy's apartment, and at 6:00 the next morning, we came back to our dorm rooms and slept all day. That night I did start, and I hit the first *nine* shots I took.

Cheryl Lucas
*Of course I was at John's first game that year. It was a some-
what unusual situation because John was taking the place of
Howard White, the team's point guard from the year before.*

White had had knee surgery after the season, and no one knew if he'd be able to come back and play. So here's this kid coming out of high school, no one knows who he is, he's a freshman, he's starting, and he comes out and nails his first nine field goals and has a great game.

People were saying afterwards that John had probably just been lucky. But the next game he had something like twenty points and a bunch of assists. By the third game, John had basically taken over the team. Tom McMillen, Lenny Elmore, and the seniors were basically looking to him to carry them through to the ACC finals.

I knew that taking acid the night before my game was a pretty stupid thing to do. But I didn't think anything of it, because I just knew I wasn't going to do that any more. And I didn't. I was around drugs at school. Everyone was. Drugs were on every campus in the country. But I wasn't really wasn't a part of it. In college, I saw a lot more drugs than I did in high school, but they didn't mean much to me. At my campus, there was drinking, of course, and heavy marijuana use. There was some use of other drugs like acid, but not much cocaine. A lot of guys I knew, including some of my teammates, used to smoke marijuana. I didn't smoke because I saw that when they did, all that happened was that they got wasted. When they were smoking, I used to get in their faces — make noises and faces — just to try to kill their high. I tried to talk to them about how they were hurting the team. I had never done anything until that acid trip. I escaped from that and I didn't ever want to do it again. I'd go out sometimes after working out or lifting weights and have a couple beers, but that was all. Alcohol and other drugs weren't a part of my life yet, I think because I still had this strong structure of other people around me.

By early spring, basketball season was over and it was time for tennis again. I had taken a full basketball scholarship, leaving the tennis program an extra scholarship for someone else to use. One day I just walked over to Doyle Royal, the tennis coach, and said, "Hey, Coach!

I'm here. I want to play." He didn't even know I was coming. Royal had done some research, so he knew I could play, but he didn't know just how well. I came out and beat everybody on the team. From then on I played number-one singles.

Cheryl Lucas

By the time the basketball season was about half over, everybody knew who John was, that he was a force to be dealt with. But when he came out and played tennis in the spring and did so well, people were really shocked. John hadn't practiced or played any tennis for almost a year. The guys on the tennis team, two in particular, had grown up in tennis and played all the time. Now John just walks in and takes over number-one singles role in the tournaments. They couldn't believe it.

I had let my tennis go for a year so I could concentrate on my basketball, and during my freshman season, I never really got my game all the way back. I won some matches, and I won the ACC doubles title, but I wasn't playing like I knew I could.

The next year, I played a little more tennis than normal during the basketball season and I won the ACC singles title. Our tennis team had a lot of charisma. We were all good, fun-loving guys who could give people a good show. Previously there had been hardly any coverage of tennis matches, and nobody came to see them. But things changed when we came, and we started getting more and more coverage.

We had a growing following, not just at Maryland, but at other schools, too. We were a bunch of guys that were very loose and very good. When we traveled, basketball fans from other cities and schools — like Clemson, North Carolina, and North Carolina State — would come to the tennis matches. We were getting crowds of eight hundred to nine hundred people — very large for tennis matches. They would just root against me because I was on Maryland's basketball team. Then in the winter, when I'd be playing basketball, people would come to the game with tennis balls and throw them at me. I had a lot of showman-ship and hotdog in me. I liked to play to the crowd. It wasn't malicious or arrogant or anything — I did it just to have some fun. That's why I could relate so much with Dennis Rodman [of the San Antonio Spurs]. I was like him in that way.

In the ACC tournament my senior year, I was getting beat by a guy named Billy Rock. I had already lost the first set badly at 6-1. Arthur Ashe's agent, Donald Dell, had come down to Maryland to watch my match. When he saw what was happening, he helped coach me through it to beat Rock for the ACC title. Donald stayed in touch during my years at Maryland, and he or one of his guys was ready to be my agent and represent me when I graduated. I went out in style my senior year winning not only the singles title, but the doubles title, too.

College was just like high school for me in many ways. The Wash-ington, D. C., area was clearly a bigger market than Durham, and I was getting a lot of national media attention, too, but this didn't feel very different to me. I'd been getting media attention for years already. I was always in the local papers — these just had larger circulation — and I had been playing tennis in front of audiences of thousands of people for years now, so the college crowds didn't intimidate me either.

The attention and special treatment all athletes get in this country started for me when people found out I was good in sports. At a young age, I noticed how athletes were treated in the world. When kids become successful, they begin to be noticed by other parents, and you see articles about them in the paper every day. Do you see that kind of attention for kids who do well academically? Hardly!

Good athletes get special treatment in many ways — and people even help make life *outside* of sports easier for you. Here's a great exam-ple. At some time during my time at Maryland, the country started gas rationing. If you had odd numbers on your plates, you could get gas on odd numbered days, and vice versa. Well, I could get gas anytime. I'd just drive into a station around town and they'd fill me up. I drove my car all over the place. This may not sound like a big deal to you if you're thirty or forty years old, but to an eighteen-year-old kid, it was big. It made a big impression on me.

Athletes also have an advantage with their social life. Everyone knows them, and everyone wants to be with them.

Cheryl Lucas

Of course all the women liked John because he was in the headlines all the time, he was popular, he talked with just about everybody, and he knew how to treat just about everybody right. He always had that knack. For some reason, people never feel threatened by him. That's not to say that everybody liked him, but he had a way of making people feel at ease.

While he was in college, the black exploitation films like Shaft *were popular, and John really liked this John Shaft character. He thought of himself as Shaft so much that it became his nickname. He even went out and bought a leather coat, turtleneck and whatever so he could look like Shaft. He tried to play the Shaft role.*

John had many girlfriends, both black and white. Women always liked him. At that time, there was really no problem with interracial dating. Not a lot did it, but if you did, it was okay. They used to have these contests in the ACC to see which guys had the best legs or the best body, and of course John's name was always mentioned. Even though he had a lot of girlfriends, my parents and I always thought he'd end up marrying Debbie because they'd known each other for so long.

Debbie Lucas

I liked John in high school, but we didn't really date then. My parents, especially my mother, didn't want me to date while I was in high school, so our opportunities to be together were pretty much limited to seeing each other around school he was always coming by my classroom or in the cafeteria to talk to me or tease me, but that was it. So I knew he liked me, too, but we didn't date. Besides, he always had other girl-friends — he was kind of a flirt.

We did date a little toward the end of our senior year in high school, but it wasn't until college that we really started seeing each other more seriously. I was going to college at North Carolina Central near Durham, and John was going to Maryland. He would come back during the term breaks and holidays, and we would go to movies and parties together. When his team had games against Duke and North Carolina, I'd go to see him play. Also, I had cousins who lived in Mary-land, so when I went up there during the school year to visit them, I would attend John's games and tennis matches. John always came back to Durham in the summer, so we saw one another a lot then.

We didn't marry right out of college. John went to Hous-ton to play pro ball, and I worked with the Durham Arts Coun-cil teaching creative movement and dance in the Durham city schools. We each had our own lives. Besides, I wasn't the kind who wanted to marry in college or right out of high school. I wanted to work for a while.

When John went to Houston after he graduated, our situ-ation was similar to when we were in college. John would drive home to visit me when he had some time off, and I would go to Houston to visit him during my breaks, too. When the Rock-ets were playing the Bullets, I'd go up to Maryland and stay with my cousins so I could watch John play. We'd also see each other in the off-season. I'd even drive down with him when he worked at basketball summer camps.

After a couple years at Maryland, my sports career was rolling. I was achieving every sports-oriented goal I had. I had also come to college for academic reasons, even though they weren't so important to me. Never-theless, I wanted to get good grades, too — that was a definite goal of mine.

As far as my studies in college were concerned, well, I did what I needed to do. I wasn't an outstanding student in college for the same reason I wasn't one in junior and senior high. Generally, there wasn't the kind of challenge I was looking for in what I did. Now if we had a debate in class about something like the Boston Tea Party, and I really had to get into the heart of it and try to defend my position on who was right or wrong, I was all for that. I was really motivated to make a strong presentation for that kind of project. The motivation, of course, was competition. If there was going to be a winner, then I could get myself going. But for the normal stuff — I didn't have the desire to work. Give me an essay question, that wasn't a challenge. I did, however, love taking multiple choice tests — especially if I didn't know the material very well. I turned it into a game — me against the teacher. I was great at developing the art of guessing. I'd try to figure out how the teacher set up the test, and if she had a system for the answers. Could I outsmart her and figure out her system? There was my challenge.

Cheryl, together with Joe Harrington, the assistant coach at Maryland at the time they recruited me, oversaw my schoolwork and made sure I did it.

Cheryl Lucas

When John came up to college, I wanted him to understand that basketball was important, but the real reason he was there was to get an education. I tried to keep him focused on his schooling and help him realize that it wasn't a life and death situation as far as ball was concerned, but he did need that education. I told John that he had been given a wonderful opportunity — a free college education — and I didn't want to see him waste it. I especially wanted him to remember who he was as a black man. You heard then of a lot of black athletes who, once they got into big white colleges, basically forgot their people. I always tried to give him a sense of his own self-worth and importance.

I only studied enough to get by, but I still maintained a 3.0 GPA in my major, which was business. I was a better student than a lot of other athletes, and I was right there in the middle of the overall student body academically. I was no Tom McMillen, who was really smart. Everybody was so jealous of how smart he was. I didn't want that. I wanted to be average. Looking back, I can see the contradiction here. It certainly didn't bother me to be the best athlete I could be, or to beat anyone I could. And it never occurred to me that people might be jealous of my skills as an athlete. But academics was in the realm of my non-sports life, and I continued to feel uncomfortable about that part of my life.

I didn't understand balance, or that a middle ground was acceptable, even though that's exactly what I wanted to have as a person. I didn't have the skills to be comfortable enough to be that person outside of sports. The only skills and principles I had were those of an athlete, which are very, very competitive.

I really want to stress this point to all parents who have kids in athletics: I don't care how talented or good they are — tell your kids when to cut the competition off. It stops as soon as the game ends. I know sometimes that's really hard, but they have to learn to do it. And as adults, we can help them learn by giving them some guidance. It's really hard for kids to know when to stop the competition.

In the past few years, a couple of famous athletes have dropped dead from heart problems. The media and others talked like this was some bizarre new occurrence. It isn't. I know, because it happened while I was in college. Two of my teammates, Owen Brown and Chris Patten, both died while I was at Maryland. Each had the same thing happen: some problem with their heart or aorta.

Owen was the first, and when he died, it was really traumatic for me. That was the first time I or any of us had lost someone close. I didn't know why something like this would happen. I wanted a reason, and the only explanation I could come up with was that it had something to do with drug use. Some guys on the team smoked marijuana, and when these guys died, I immediately thought that marijuana might have played a part. Of course it didn't, but I thought it did. It was another reason why I never used those drugs in college.

I had to speak at both of their funerals, and I remember having a hard time coming up with something to say. It was a really, really a strange time. At that age, we never imagine we can die. I can see now, however, that these deaths, and that of a friend in high school who got killed one night trying to pass a truck, bothered me, but they didn't really touch me. I didn't let painful things get to me. I guess you could say I thought about these deaths some, but that was all. I just went on with my life. I used alcohol a little more to cover the pain — though I didn't see that that was what I was doing — and I concentrated on playing ball. My attitude was, "Life goes on." I didn't have a clue about the value of life. I took it so much for granted, just like I took so many things for granted then. I had no idea what I had.

During my first two years at Maryland, we had a great team with Tom McMillen, Lenny Elmore, Mo Howard, Owen Brown, Chris Patten, and others. We were considered the UCLA of the East in basketball, and at the time, UCLA had won nine of the last ten national championships. They were incredible. We thought we could take the NCAA championship during one of those years, but we couldn't get out of the ACC either year. The NCAA tournament hadn't yet changed to the current sixty-four-team format.

Lefty Driesell

John was a great leader both on and off the court, as well as a great athlete. He was a very unselfish and smart player who always played hard. We had a tremendous team then at Maryland. John was the leading scorer in the ACC tournament as a freshman. We were in the Top Ten every year he was there, but we never won the NCAA tournament with him. We lost in his freshman year to North Carolina State 103-101 — a game everybody says was the greatest ever played in an ACC tournament. NC State went on to win the national championship that year. John played a great game.

He was very popular with everybody on campus, too. Usually in college tennis nobody comes to see the games,

*but when he was playing, the stands would be full. He was
good, of course, but people liked him, too. He was just a fine
young man. John's dad always used to send this little thing
from his church with thoughts for each day of the week — a
little thing to help you get through the day. John used to read
those to the team. He was the last person I ever thought
would have a problem with drugs.*

After two years, Tom McMillen and Lenny Elmore graduated, and we
needed another big-time player to take McMillen's place inside. During
my sophomore year, Maryland began recruiting Moses Malone. We all
believed that if we could get Mo, we'd have an NCAA title.

I spent a lot of time with Mo that year. I'd be going down to Peters-
burg, Virginia, to see him where he was living. Moses had a mystique
about him that was really, really special, and we became good friends.
Finally Moses decided to come to Maryland. The first day of school, I
went to meet him, and I said, "Mo let's get ready to go to class." "I don't
want to go to class," he said, "because I'm going to go to the pros." I
was stunned. After not even one day at school, Mo goes pro.

I was really down about this. I told him not to tell anyone, and I
went and got all our guys together and had a meeting in Lefty's office.
After I told them what Mo was going to do, we came up with a plan to
get him to stay. We were each getting fifteen dollars a month for laun-
dry money and whatever, so I said, "Come on guys, let's each give Mo
our fifteen dollars." We did it to see if we could get him to stay. Can
you believe how stupid I was! Mo was getting $300,000 a year at least,
and we were going to give him a hundred and fifty bucks! I still laugh
about this incident!

Mo did, of course, go to the pros. He signed with the Utah Jazz,
who were coached that year by Tom Nissalke. Our year was okay; we
did the best we could, but we just weren't capable of going very far.
Once Moses went pro, I didn't see him again until we got to play
together at Houston.

Moses' decision to turn pro early disappointed me a lot. Ironically,

I was faced with a similar decision only a few months later in my junior year. What started everything was a decision by the coaches to move me from point guard to small forward to make room in the backcourt for a kid by the name of Brad Davis. I didn't liked the idea at all because Mo Howard and I had been playing so well together in the backcourt that we were called the best backcourt in the country one year. What's more, I didn't like the idea of playing small forward. Even worse, agents and other people were telling me that because my natural position was point guard, I'd lose some of my value in the draft by playing out of that position.

Then what do you know — that year the New Jersey Nets of the ABA [the American Basketball Association, which merged with the NBA less than two years later] made me their number-one pick. They were offering me a $1 million contract to come out after my junior year. The money, together with the moves by the team, had me really tempted to follow Moses' example.

I didn't know what to do. That was *so* much money at the time — the equivalent of a $5-million or $6-million contract today. I needed some advice so I called Donald Dell, my agent, and then, the day before I had to sign, I called my parents. My dad told me to think about it and pray on it. And my mother...well she had always played an important role in my life, but to me she always seemed to be more in the background, behind my dad. This was the first her own strength really appeared to me coming straight from her. I knew it was there, but it always came through my father. She finally stepped out from behind him. Late that night she called me back and said, "Son, there's only one thing you ever promised me you'd do, and that is to get your degree. I love you. See you later." Then she hung up the phone.

Blond Lucas

John called to tell us that he was very close to turning pro because he could get so much money. "Well," I said, "the choice is yours. But you will have to live with that choice. Everybody in the family has been to school. You'll be the only one in the family without a degree. You have to think about that. Those are things you might look back at and wonder about when you're older. Was this the best thing you could have done?" He told me he'd make a decision soon, and I said, "It's your choice, you make it." This was very late at night.

The next morning he called and said, "Momma, did you sleep last night?" I said, "Yeah, I told you, the choice is yours, not mine. Why should I be losing any sleep?" And then he said, "You know I'm not going to drop out of school." So I knew that for him the money wasn't worth it.

After that conversation, what choice did I have? None. I'd made a promise. I had to keep it. I stayed in school and went back for my senior year. I knew I had good value in either league now anyway, because agents were calling me up and telling me that I could go number one or number two in the draft if I declared hardship. The hardship rule (which is no longer in effect) prevented NBA teams from drafting college players before their senior years unless they could prove financial hardship to justify needing the salary. Well, I wasn't no hardship guy. I could have made hardship, but I wanted that degree in business administration. And little did I know at the time how I would eventually get to use that degree.

My senior year seemed to pass by pretty quickly, and suddenly it was my last basketball game as a Terrapin. That was another really sad, bitter time, a kind of dying for me. It was exactly the same feeling I had on graduating from high school — a feeling of terrible emptiness, not knowing what the future had in store for me, facing another big, big change in my life and not wanting to make it.

Even today I say that I could go back to high school. Why? Because it was a time when I didn't have any responsibilities — and this is what made it so hard for me to get sober. I had to take responsibility for my whole life, and I hadn't ever had to do that. Everything was always done for me all my life. This is the special life of the good athlete.

On the basketball team, everything is taken care of for you. You don't have to find a place to live, you stay in the dorm or in an apartment they find for you — and pay for. You don't have to cook; you eat with the team. Need some new shoes? Tell the coach, and someone will get them for you. You don't even have to wash your clothes; after the practice, you put them in a bag, and they wash them for you. The next day you have clean clothes. It's great — but the problem is, you don't learn any responsibility.

I had always had mothers, fathers, sisters, and brothers in sports. It was like a family: my coach became my father, my trainer became my mother, the assistant coaches were my aunts and uncles. And whichever coach recruited you, he became like a doting aunt, you were his favorite. He wants to see you succeed because he brought you there.

I was naive about the reality of college sports. When I first came to Maryland, I was really moved by how much the coaches and everybody seemed to care. It made me feel I was special. After a couple years, however, I began seeing that the same letters I had received as a recruit were now going out to other kids. I thought the letters I'd gotten were special letters, personal letters to me. Then I saw that they were essentially form letters. I actually went to talk about this to my coaches, and they said something like, "Well, we do care about you." I didn't understand. I didn't know what to think, but I knew it didn't feel right. I was only beginning to understand that time passed, that guys came and went; I did see, though, that the new guys coming in are your enemy because you're in competition against one another. But I just didn't see the bigger picture. I didn't understand the *business* side of athletics. I thought basketball at Maryland would die when I left. I figured I would compete, play hard, and be the best. Then, when I graduated, I would have been so good that it would never be the same there without me.

Bob Bass, former vice president of basketball operations, San Antonio Spurs

I first started watching John Lucas the last year of the ABA when John was a senior at the University of Maryland. The NCAA tennis championships were in Corpus Christi, Texas, that year. Being the outstanding tennis player that he was, John came down to play in the tournament .

While he was there, we invited him up to San Antonio to talk to him about playing for the Spurs, who were then in the ABA. We wanted to sign him to a contract right then. After the tournament, we had an interview with him that even included the owner of the club, and John said he'd give our offer some thought.

Sometime in May or early June, the two leagues merged, and as part of the agreement, ABA teams were not allowed a draft choice. Even if we had signed John to a contract before the merger, it would have been voided under the terms of the agreement.

It was a shame, too, because we really wanted him. John was the best point guard in all of college basketball. It's really unusual for a smaller point guard like John, at 6' 3", to be ranked number one in the draft. Someone bigger like Magic Johnson, at 6' 9" — that's more common. The top two or three spots always go to big people. That John was ranked number one showed what people thought about him as a player.

At Maryland there had never been a bigger star than me. I don't mean that in a boastful way; that's the way it was. In my senior yearbook, I wrote that my ambition was to be the first black president of the United States. What a goal! I always wanted to be the best — to go right to the top. And the next goal was to be a professional basketball player and a professional tennis player. The reality, of course, is that only X number of guys make it to college or to the pros, but everybody still thinks they're going to make the next level. And I was no different. Two of my teammates had graduated and went on to play in the pros, so, I said, if they made it, so can I. But for me, the key here is that my dream *did* happen for me. My dreams kept becoming reality.

While I was waiting to see what would happen to me in the ABA and NBA drafts, I decided to sign a professional contract to play World Team Tennis. I headed out to California to play tennis the summer after graduation with the Golden Gate Gators. Frew McMillan and Tom Okker, the Flying Dutchman, were on my team. And I was excited to be back in California, the site of my Davis Cup victory.

CHAPTER 5

PRO CAREER

The NBA scheduled their draft for early summer, and I was having a hard time waiting for the big day. During most of my senior year, I'd been telling my friends and teammates that I'd be the number-one pick in the draft, but you never really know about these things. Two days before the draft, I was playing basketball in the gym when I got a call from my agent, Donald Dell. He told me, "John, get your suit and tie, and buy yourself a ticket for the next flight to Houston. I'll meet you there tomorrow night."

Tom Nissalke

During John's senior year in college, I was working for the Utah Jazz of the ABA. One of my main jobs was to identify the best guards in the country and follow them around the league to evaluate their skills. There were four I was watching that year: John Lucas of Maryland, Quinn Buckner of Indiana, Armond Hill of Princeton, and Ronnie Lee, who was playing at Oregon State. As I got to know them, it became apparent that John and Quinn were the two best.

In one of those curious turns of fate, the Houston Rockets hired me to be their head coach just two days before the draft. We weren't necessarily in the market for a guard, although we felt by then that John was the best guard available. Then we learned that Atlanta was certain they wanted to take Robert Parish, so we made a trade to pick first in the draft — and we decided to make John Lucas our pick.

John and Donald Dell came down to Houston the night before the draft. Ray Patterson [Houston's general manager], John, Dell, and I stayed up all night and got the deal done. It was pretty dramatic, actually.

The next day at the draft, the news raced through the pro community: "The Houston Rockets have drafted and signed the number-one pick in the NBA draft this year — John Lucas of the University of Maryland."

Going as the number-one pick didn't awe me much because I felt I deserved it. I'd been telling everybody I was the best guard in the country. I'd been number one throughout my career, so why should things be different now? I'd been expecting this for so long that it just didn't feel that big.

That summer I played World Team Tennis while I waited to go to the Rockets' training camp. I didn't really know what to expect out of pro life and pro basketball, but I was really excited about going to Houston. It was a completely new environment. Deep down, I didn't know if I would be able to make it as a pro player, but I knew that I would work really hard, and hard work had always paid off for me in the past.

At this time, I also ran into one very big and completely unexpected change from high school and college: for the first time in my life, I was completely on my own. I had my own apartment and was living alone. I'd never done that before. Suddenly, I no longer had that structure of family and friends around me; there was only me. I did all right with it that summer because of tennis and travel and whatever. I thought I could handle it and I was okay, but life felt really different. And when the season started, I was *very* excited about being a pro player.

Tom Nissalke

When John came in the fall of 1976, he was a very self-confident young guy. He'd started working out in the preseason, and you could tell that he had a lot of ability. He was coming to a team whose better players had been playing together for three or four years. They were a pretty good team, but they really hadn't gone anywhere. What's more, everybody had their roles — and their personal rivalries — and then suddenly this rookie who's the number-one pick shows up. The team was a bit resentful of John at first. They felt, Here's the number-one pick getting all the publicity, and he hasn't demonstrated yet that he can even play at the pro level.

We went through the exhibition season and were pretty good. John was starting to fit in as a backup to Calvin Murphy. Early in the regular season, however, we were able to make a deal for Moses Malone, whom I had coached when I was with the Jazz. It wasn't until then that the guys really saw what could be done. All the pieces fell into place, and we had almost an ideal team. Now John was right in his element. Other players saw that he liked to pass the ball, and once the players saw that John could make the plays, they realized that he was going to make the rest of them look better.

The final piece was Moses, who was just a terrific guy and a terrific talent. He was a very withdrawn fellow, though — still a young kid only in his second year in pro ball. John and Moses had known each other for a couple of years and were good friends, so they were excited to play together. John, besides being a good player in his own right, performed double duty by getting Moses to come out of his shell.

When the season started, I didn't. It was the first time in my whole career that I wasn't a starter. My role was to come off the bench and back Calvin Murphy. After twenty-eight games or so, I began to start.

Then Moses Malone and I got back together. Nissalke — the same guy who "stole" Moses from me a year ago at Maryland — had been telling me that they were trying to get him. Mo eventually signed. He moved into the apartment above me, and we became very good friends.

I worked hard that season, but I didn't really know what to expect. Playing for the first time on courts I'd only seen on TV against guys I'd always looked up to — Dr. J in the Spectrum, Walt Frazier and Earl Monroe at Madison Square Garden, Kareem and the Lakers in the Forum — everything was very exciting at first.

Pretty soon, however, I woke up to the reality of pro ball. The glamour and excitement wear off quickly. It's a job, and being a player in the NBA in those years was really brutal. For one thing, we would play three or four games back-to-back — Thursday through Sunday, for example — and then the league would show them later in the week via tape delay. We were playing at crazy times, and it was very, very exhausting. Travel was much more extensive then, too. The league was nothing like it is today.

While it was certainly new and exciting to be a pro player, basketball was a much different environment than what I was accustomed to in college. I was shocked and disappointed to find that there wasn't the same kind of camaraderie on the team. The guys didn't go out to eat after the games; we went our separate ways. The wives didn't talk to one another much. There wasn't any big booster club. Nobody met us at the airport when we came back from a road trip. I was used to playing in front of sold-out arenas, and ours wasn't. I was used to basketball being king, but in Houston, football was. Basketball was on the third page of the sports section.

I really liked Houston, but I was very lonely. And I had so much idle time. Practice was an hour and a half a day, and then we were through until the next time we practiced or had a game. Suddenly I wasn't able to fill up my life with sports. What's more, there were no classes to go to, no campus to hang around. Just me and my apartment. Needless to say, I really looked forward to games.

Tom Nissalke

We had a very good season that year. We won our division and went to the semifinals, eventually losing to Philadelphia in six games. Portland won it all that year, and had we gotten to the finals, we probably would have won the whole thing, because we beat Portland three out of four times during the season.

John was one of the top rookies. He wasn't what I would consider a great student of the game then, and I used to tell him, "Well, John, the big guy is going to have to study this game sometime." But he really didn't need to yet because he was with good players and the game came pretty easily to him. He was twenty-two years old, a good-looking guy, a solid person — always upbeat, always fun to be around. He had a certain cockiness about him that wasn't offensive. He was very well liked. And there was never any suspicion of drugs or drinking to excess. I don't recall John ever doing more than drinking a beer then.

After my first year as a pro basketball player, I played professional tennis again in the summer with the New Orleans Nets. My doubles partner was a woman by the name of Renee Richards. We made quite a team — I was the only black player in the league, and she was the only transsexual!

Also at this time, I got involved a bit more with drugs. I'd tried cocaine for the first time during my senior year in college, right before graduation, and now I tried it again. I really, really enjoyed coke, but I wasn't overusing. I was just experimenting and having fun.

Though I didn't know it at the time, what was really happening to me was that I was running out of athletic goals. I simply didn't see anything else to reach for — so I began reaching for drugs and alcohol instead. In an article about me in the paper then, I was talking about other things I wanted to do — be president of the United States, be a hockey player, whatever. Looking back, I can see that was a strong sign I was becoming bored.

I was running out of challenges. I was becoming a one-dimensional being. Basketball and tennis had become who I was rather than what I did. I didn't know who I was. What do you like to do in your spare time? Watch basketball. What do you do when you ain't watching basketball? Well, I play it. What do you do when you're not playing basketball? Oh, definitely I'm playing some tennis. What do you do when you don't have a tennis match? Well, I'm thinking about tennis. I had become an adult in sports, but I was still a child in the rest of life. I was twenty-two years old, and sports was really all I'd done. I had other choices, but I didn't see them. I had a good education, but I put it aside — it was put up on the shelf, tucked away and forgotten.

I think today about all the kids who say, "Okay, what's really important is to try to be a really good athlete." Well, here I was, someone who did all that and got as good as anybody could get, and then still found that it wasn't enough to make a life. I was going to have to have another life sometime; sports couldn't be everything forever. But I didn't know that then. I thought I was going to be dead at thirty-five. I thought I'd be in basketball heaven. You might laugh at how naive this was, but I'm serious. I didn't know nothing else — and as I began to get older, I began to get scared. What the hell? What am I going to do?

I continued to play tennis, travel, have fun, and experiment with drugs that summer because I had free time and nothing better to do. It seemed harmless at the time. That fall, I came back to camp and I was drinking heavier. I wasn't taking care of my body as well as I should have been, but it hadn't had any effect on me yet.

I had made the NBA All-Rookie team, and when I began my second year with the Rockets, the 1977-78 season, I was a starter. We were all very optimistic. Everybody was back and healthy, we were used to playing together, and we thought we could have a terrific year. We had a good exhibition season, but midway into the season, things started to unravel.

The biggest blow came as the result of just that — a blow to the face of one of our key guys, Rudy Tomjonavich. We were playing the Lakers. Rudy and one of their guys, Kevin Washington, had been going at it, and Washington was really pissed. After a score, Rudy was coming back down the court when Kevin wheeled around and nailed Rudy with a monstrous punch square in the face. Just decked him. Rudy went down right in the middle of the court.

We were all angry about the incident, but we didn't think too much of it until after the game when the Laker coach, Jerry West, came in the locker room and told us how bad it was. Rudy's face had been just crushed — all kinds of breaks. He was already in the hospital and getting ready for surgery. Not only was he out for the season, we weren't sure if he'd ever play again. Kevin had almost killed him.

I think we went to Portland the next night to play, and everyone was in a daze. We just got blown out up there. Next thing we knew, Moses Malone broke his leg. Mike Newlin went down with an injury, too. It got so we never knew who would be next, and by then we were really struggling. Five of our seven top guys were out. We were down to only me and Calvin Murphy, and we just couldn't compete. We went from fifty-five wins the year before to about twenty-eight wins.

Tom Nissalke

We were not a very good team that year. We just couldn't overcome losing half our guys to injuries. The thing I always remember about John that year, though, was how much we used to talk about strategy, about what would work against the different teams and defenses.

One night we played Indiana and beat them in a great game. John came to me toward the end of the game, so full of enthusiasm. He had had twenty assists. He was absolutely terrific, and he said to me, "Coach, I think I'm finally starting to get the hang of this game." I just laughed. He'd been great for two years, but he was absolutely brilliant that night. He ended up second in the league in assists that year.

During the off-season, I was really looking forward to the next year. We knew Rudy and Moses would both be back. We felt that we had the makings of a mini-dynasty if everyone could stay healthy. We had talent and a lot of really nice guys.

I was totally unaccustomed to losing, and we lost so many games that year. It was terrible, especially after such a good first year. Being on a losing team made everything seem different. I began to miss some practices as I got more involved with alcohol and other drugs, but I didn't miss any games.

Toward the end of the season, rumors began circulating that Houston was trying to make a deal with Golden State for Rick Barry. I didn't think much of it, except that if we had Barry, we could be unbeatable. At this time, however, the NBA's trade rules included a policy they called "fair compensation." This meant that if we got Barry, the Warriors would get someone as compensation from Houston. I remember wondering who that would be.

Tom Nissalke

In the summer, I started to hear more rumors that we were dealing with the possibility of our getting Rick Barry. As the coach, I had no input at all in management decisions, so I was as much in the dark as everyone else. I had nothing to do with this deal. Everyone kept saying that Barry could be a plus for our team, but my thought was that we better know what the compensation was going to be before we did it. We definitely didn't want to give up Moses or John, and we didn't think they'd go for Calvin Murphy.

Finally, word came out that Barry had signed with us. But the Rockets hadn't determined the compensation — and that turned out to be a big mistake. Then came a night I'll never forget. I was eating dinner in a Houston restaurant when I got word that the compensation was going to be John Lucas. Tears came to my eyes. I was completely floored. We were losing a terrific player who was only going to get even better — and a guy who had become a friend. I had really become close to John personally, and my family absolutely loved him. He was great to my kids.

I called John, and I mean he was really hurt. He loved

this team and he'd found a home in Houston. He couldn't believe something like this could happen. He wanted to know how I could do this to him. He just didn't believe that as the coach I had nothing to do with it.

I was absolutely beside myself. We had a good team that should have been good for many years. We just didn't have very strong ownership. Neither player wanted the trade — both were being forced to leave places where they were well liked. And for John, he was leaving a situation in Houston where everybody lived fairly close to one another and where everybody got along — the coaches, the players — everyone liked one another. The Bay area would be very different.

Blond Lucas

In the latter part of John's second year at Houston, we became aware that something was going on with John because articles were coming out of Houston about his missing practices. We didn't know the what or the why, but we knew something odd was happening. When John was traded to Golden State, it was a shocking experience for him. He felt he had done well, and then he gets traded. I think it takes a strong constitution to go through something like that, regardless of the person. We look back on this trade as one of the things that helped push him over the edge.

The 1978-79 season was beginning, and there I was in Golden State. I had mixed feelings about the move. I was further away from my family and starting over again in another city — and all my feelings of loneliness were back. Mostly, though, I thought I had died and gone to heaven because I thought it would be great to be in California. I went out with guys I'd always idolized. It was beautiful. I'd been traded for their star player, and I took over the star role. I didn't want to leave Houston, but it was okay. I had a really good season, averaging sixteen or seventeen points a game and getting a lot of assists. But I was going farther and farther out with my drug use. Cocaine was easily available everywhere now — even in Durham. It wasn't just a West Coast fad anymore.

In the late 1970s and 1980s, a fair number of people in the NBA were using drugs. That shouldn't surprise anyone, because there were a hell of a lot of other people using drugs in this country then, too. Coke was everywhere. Hell, it was all over Wall Street and middle America. Why should it be any different in the NBA?

I returned for the 1979-80 season with a full blown addiction — and I returned to a team on which about 75 percent of the players were using drugs regularly. We didn't think anything of it, though, because everybody at that time thought it was fashionable — and drugs like cocaine weren't considered addictive. It was the drug of choice for the rich and famous, so a lot of people were involved — and it was very easy to obtain.

Cheryl Lucas

John and I had never been around drugs before, neither in Durham nor at Maryland. We didn't walk over winos or drug addicts going to school and coming home. Our parents didn't drink. This was something relatively new. That second year with the Warriors, I started to hear that John was missing planes, practices, and even games, and that the crowd of people he was hanging around with was a little shady. I began to get a little concerned. When John got traded for Rick Barry, he really got involved with the whole West Coast lifestyle.

Tom Nissalke

John and I kept in touch after he went to Golden State. I was hearing rumors that he was running with some questionable people. Late in his second season with the Warriors, they were in Houston for a game. John and I went out to dinner after the game, and John brought some of these guys. It was a different crowd than I'd ever seen him with in Houston. I've always been very frank with him, and I told him that I didn't like the looks of them. I was on his case, telling him, "John, just know who your damn friends are," but he was very defensive about it.

During my second and third seasons at Golden State, 1979-80 and 1980-81, I simply lost my drive to succeed. What was there to work toward? I'd *always* been on winning teams, and we weren't. This was really hard for me to accept. Money wasn't a goal, either, because I had a three-year contract with the Warriors. I got paid the same no matter how I played. Before, I had always had another level to go to, something to strive for, but not now. In my third year, I started missing practices, blaming it on all sorts of things — and I missed some games, too.

I was clearly struggling with my life, and then tragedy struck. Coach Easterling fell dead from a heart attack minutes after visiting my parents. I had no sooner returned to the Bay area after his funeral, when my grandmother, with whom I had always been very close, died suddenly and unexpectedly. Not long after that, doctors discovered that my mother had cancer, and then my dad fell ill as well. In a very short time, of the four people I was closest to in the world, two died and two were very ill.

I never liked feeling painful emotions, and I had discovered that whenever I felt pain, sorrow, or hurt, drugs would take those feelings away. They seemed to make it all seem secondary. So that's what I did. I medicated my pain with cocaine and alcohol. I was really emotionless during what was — or should have been — a very emotional time. Until I went to treatment, I had never let myself grieve for the deaths of my grandmother and Coach Easterling. Today, fortunately, I can let myself feel my emotions. I don't fear them anymore.

John Lucas, Sr.
Everything had gone so well in our family for many years —

we didn't have any real problems, no big challenges. Then John came to what we refer to as the rough side of the mountain, the place where life gets difficult. The trade and the deaths of his grandmother and Coach Easterling hit John very, very hard. A series of difficulties just overtook him. What's more, he was still looking for his title — this elusive basketball title. And after leaving Houston, where it was in his grasp, well, he had to watch that chance slip away, too.

Here I was, Golden State's star player, the guy they'd gotten for their superstar, missing games, practices, and even the team flights. The media — even the national guys — were on this story. People couldn't figure out what was happening because this type of behavior was so uncharacteristic of me. Rumors began to circulate that I had a cocaine problem — no public accusations, just suspicions.

With about twenty games left in the season, I missed another practice and got suspended for a game. I came back, missed again, and they suspended me without pay for the rest of the year. Just like that: out of a job and out of money.

After years of knowing one another, Debbie and I had finally gotten married, but she and my daughter, Tarvia, were still living back East at this time. I was just feeling tired of living, so my solution was to ask them to move out to California. I thought having them with me all the time would help me feel better and stop using.

Debbie Lucas

I had no idea John was using drugs at this time because he never did them in front of me. But as soon as we moved to California, something about John started to seem odd. He would give me money to buy groceries or do things with, and what I didn't use right away I would just put down on the dresser, the table, or somewhere in the house. Next thing I'd know, it would be gone. John would say, "Maybe you put it in your purse or somewhere." He had me thinking I'd misplaced it.

Little things just kept happening, and I knew I wasn't going crazy, so after about four months, I figured out that something was going on. I started paying close attention to him. I noticed he was going into bathrooms and staying for a while. I started searching around a little, and I'd find cocaine. I'd been noticing that his mannerisms were different than usual. He was fidgety and paranoid; his eyes and mouth were dry. I suddenly realized what was going on — he was using. All this took a while for me to figure out because John wasn't a daily drug user. He might use on a weekend or for a few days, and then not touch it for a few weeks. When he went home to Durham, he was a different person because he didn't use there — yet. It was like living with a whole different person from the man I'd known all those years and finally married. I began to think, "What did I get myself into?"

My parents were starting to get really worried about me, too. They'd been seeing stuff in the paper, and like everyone else who knew me, they couldn't understand what was happening.

After my suspension, I decided to go back home to North Carolina to visit my parents. There was a lot of cocaine in Durham now, too. It was easy to find friends to use with, but I was worried about using with other people. I began to use in secret by myself because I didn't want to let anybody know that the things that were being said about me were true. I was getting more paranoid. Since I was staying with my parents, they began to see that something was happening with me, but they did not know what it was.

John Lucas, Sr.

Blond and I were getting quite concerned by now. When I heard on the radio one day that John had missed his plane from Oakland to Portland, I called to see what was happening.

I questioned him, and he said, "Daddy, sometimes if you're confronted, you just have to work things out for yourself. At some point I need to grow up. I know you want me to be a person of integrity — I'll take care of it." I said, "Well, that's right, but I wish you wouldn't bring that kind of scare to me."

We finally began to realize that something might be really wrong when we saw the difference in his personality when he came back to stay with us in Durham. John had always been a free spirit, very outgoing and open. But now he didn't seem very happy anymore, he didn't seem to be enjoying his life — and John always loved life. But now he was less spirited and more withdrawn.

Cheryl Lucas

John's coach at Golden State, Al Attles, called my parents about John. They had followed Al's career as a player at North Carolina A & T, and they knew him personally, too. Al felt he had to tell them there seemed to be trouble and that he was concerned. By now, I was in a bad place. John had been back East over the last couple of summers in the off-season, and we'd been to some parties where I'd seen him using cocaine. So I knew he was using — but not how much. My parents, however, didn't know a thing about it, and I didn't want to be the one to disappoint them by telling them he had a drug problem. On the other hand, how could they help John if they didn't know he was having a problem?

Even though my attorneys, my agent, my sister — practically everybody — was saying I had a drug and alcohol problem, I didn't think I did. I was in strong denial. Drugs were having an effect, but I couldn't see that they were the problem. I thought the Bay area was the problem and that I needed to go somewhere else, so I asked the Warriors to trade me. I was trying the geographic cure.

In the meantime, my attorneys were trying to get me a job with another team. Before the season had ended, the Cleveland Cavaliers were interested in me, so interested that they were willing to give me the first $2-million-a-year contract in basketball. This is when the money boom began to hit in pro basketball. But before we could sign the deal, I got suspended and they backed out.

While I was back in Durham, my agent, David Falk, had contacted the New Jersey Nets, and they showed an interest in me. Two days before I was to sign a contract for around $300,000 for the next year, I was stopped in Durham for a DWI. It made the back page of the paper in Durham, and somebody from the Nets apparently heard about it. They dumped the deal.

By this time Falk was really pressing me about my drug use. I finally agreed to have an evaluation done and checked myself into a hospital in Washington. For five days I went through a whole battery of tests to see if I had an addiction. Well, I got a clean bill of health. No mental problems, no nothing. And yet here I was doing cocaine almost every day that ended in *y*. Well, I knew I had some kind of problem, but this test just reinforced my belief that the problem wasn't drugs. I still thought I could stop using anytime I wanted.

Cheryl Lucas

People get involved with drugs to begin with because it's an outlet. It's something that makes them feel good in the beginning. Nobody feels bad until they become addicted. People act like folks just decide to go out and get on drugs and lose their jobs, lose their families and everything. A lot of times it's a process that gets worse slowly. It becomes part of a person's very life. It's not something that happens overnight.

That's what was happening to John. When he was out in Golden State, people said to him, "How could you let all that money go?" It's not about money, and it's not something that you just decide to do. There's a reason that people get high. Something's not there in their life. Look at John. He had an education. He wasn't a poor, black, ghetto kid who didn't know better, or whose dad taught him to smoke weed. Whatever John had set out to do in his life, he was able to do. It's really eerie. Somehow he always found a way to be successful, and I think he probably thought he was going to be a successful addict, until his use got out of control.

After the Nets backed out of that deal, I spent the winter living and working out in Maryland while I looked for a new club. Not long before the 1981-82 season, I signed a contract to play with the Utah Jazz, who were being coached now by Tom Nissalke. But because Golden State had the first right of refusal, they had fifteen days to match the Jazz's offer. During this waiting period, Kevin Porter of the Washington Bullets tore his Achilles tendon — and the Bullets made a deal to get me to take Porter's place.

I just couldn't believe my luck! I'm a Bullet, I'm back in my hometown, I'm excited as I can be. I'm thinking, This isn't a new place to me, I'm living here and I'll have all the structure I had in my past around me again. I'm back home. Things are going to be all right.

But it didn't make a damn bit of difference, because I was way out in left field. I was very good at first, but then I missed some practices. I missed a couple games. I didn't know what was wrong, but I certainly didn't think alcohol or drugs was the problem. I thought everybody else was the problem — Debbie, my kid, Cheryl, my family.

That Christmas — and I'll never forget this incident — my parents came up to see me before a game. When we got to the arena, a guy I bought drugs from was waiting for me. He saw that I had my parents with me, but he didn't care at all. He just came up to me and demanded to know about his money. I told him I would get him his money. My father kept asking me who these people were that I was hanging out with. Of course I lied to him. My addiction had me lying and covering it up all the time. I had lost all sense of my values. I just couldn't believe I was lying to my parents, two people I loved dearly and respected a great deal. But I was. I had no conscience.

Debbie Lucas

When John started having problems after he joined the Bullets, they tried to keep it hidden. When he missed practices or came late to a game, they would say that John was having domestic problems. Well, domestic problems weren't the problem; the problem was that he was out on a binge and didn't get back home in time to get ready for practice. Or if he had gotten home, he was in no condition to go to practice. I let John use me for a while, I know, but I didn't know what to do to help him. And the league didn't either. At that time, no one knew what to do with a player on drugs.

Then things started getting even worse. Terrible, actually. John would stay out late, sometimes for a day or even more. He'd come back late at night or early the next morning just filthy — beer spilled all over him, smelling of urine. He'd come in and he'd walk through the house like he was looking for something. He wouldn't fuss or say anything to me, he'd just go and take a shower and go to sleep. He was never violent, though he sometimes said something ugly that would hurt my feelings. After his sleep, he would be so sorry about what he'd done that he would try to make it up to us. Sometimes he would buy the kids three or four hundred dollars worth of toys trying to make up for what he'd done. One month, he totaled both our cars.

I knew the type of person he really was — very soft and caring — and I knew that this wasn't him. He was like a little lost child. I just kept being patient and praying, and got a lot of help from my family to keep me going.

The Bullets, Debbie, my family — they were helping me in the only way they knew, which was to keep my using hidden as much as possible. I had been screwing up too badly with the Bullets, though, and it was inevitable that a story on me would break.

David DuPree, sportswriter for *USA Today*

I was covering the Bullets for the Washington Post, *and when John came to the team from Golden State, I already knew about the cocaine problem. I'd heard from people inside the game that it was a given that he was using. Our editor had heard this, too, and he wanted me to do a story to that effect. I refused, saying that there was no proof, and that I wouldn't go out on a witch hunt.*

I then went to John and told him that I knew he was using, but that it wasn't really any of my business. I said I wouldn't write anything unless he started missing games or it affected his play. "That's the best I can do," I said. "I have a job to do and you got a job to do — and if what you do affects me, I'm going to have to say something. Other than that, I don't care." John said, "Fine," and that was it.

Maybe a couple of months after that conversation, John missed a game in Philadelphia. There was no obvious reason for it. The team, however, was basically okay with that, and they said, "Well, it happens to everybody." Then he missed another one, and when I saw him later, he looked really messed up again.

Here's how bad things had gotten. I was with a friend in New York, after a Bullets game. We were walking near the hotel where the Bullets used to stay, when we noticed a group of four or five Bullets walking toward us. The woman I was with wasn't a big basketball fan, and she said, "God, those guys are big!" When I told her they were players on the Bullets, she said, "But who's that little old man following them?" That "little old man" was John, wearing a knit hat and a long tattered coat. She just couldn't believe he was a ballplayer. He was in his twenties and he looked like a fifty-year-old man.

I just couldn't ignore what was going on any longer, so before their next home game, I took John aside and told him that we had had an agreement, and that now it looked like we had a problem. I said to him, "You can go and talk to your lawyer or your agent, and you can speak your piece. We can do this in whatever way is best for you, but I have to write the story.

It was common knowledge around the league that lots of guys were using — but everyone was being careful enough that they didn't have to do anything about it. George Gervin was a user, but whenever Ice was messed up or whatever, he would just call and say he was sick and couldn't come in to play. And when he did come to the game, he'd always get his thirty points. He never brought embarrassment to the club or the league. A lot of guys were like that. I guess I was the first who just couldn't do it.

After DuPree approached me with the news that he was going to write the story, I got together with Donald Falk and we decided to go public. This was really the first admission of drug use by an NBA player, the first time that the NBA ever admitted publicly that there was a drug problem in the league. Until then, I don't think they really understood the extent of the problem, but they didn't really want to find out, either.

My story made front page news in the *Washington Post* and went all over the country. I was the one who forced the NBA to admit they had trouble with drugs. Before I could play another game, I had to go see Commissioner Lawrence O'Brien. The problem he and the league had was that they didn't have any drug policies or procedures like we have today. They didn't know what to do with me. Falk and I had our strategy ready when we walked into our meeting.

The Commissioner showed me a stack of newspapers from all over the country with headlines like "Lucas Hooked on Coke." He said, "What can I do about this?" Falk and I told him that this was something I used to do, but didn't do anymore. We told him he couldn't very well punish me for something I wasn't doing anymore! After I promised that I would go seek help at the end of the year, they let me go back to the Bullets.

After that, what I was saying to reporters and other people was this: "Okay, I'm tired. I'm tired of running, of trying to hide my problem. Everybody is thinking I have a drug problem. Well, I do. I have a drug problem. Now just leave me alone. And when I do screw up, now you know why. I'm going to fight this thing as best I can, and now that you know what's going on, leave me alone." People didn't know how to respond to that, so they let me be.

I had always been a god in the Washington area, so when I came back to play that season, no one knew how to react. What they'd been hearing about me in the papers and on TV was so different from who I was and what I had done when I was at Maryland. People had thought I just wasn't the type of guy who could have an alcohol or coke problem. When I played, I didn't get booed or cheered. The fans simply didn't do anything.

I finished out the 1981-82 season. I still had some problems — I missed a flight once — but I didn't miss any more games. The Bullets even hired two bodyguards to keep up with me, to make sure I got to my practices and games. These guys actually lived at our house. But I still used to find a way to slip out on them or trick them or whatever. The team just kept pacifying me and trying to figure out what to do with me.

By the end of the season, though, everybody was tired of me and my problems. One day in the locker room after a game, I admitted to having a problem. I asked each one of my teammates for help. Now the guys who'd done drugs with me understood what I was saying, but how could they help? I was so naive. They all agreed to help me, but of course I didn't get any better.

I reluctantly agreed to go get professional help. I entered an out-patient program down in Virginia, but I didn't put any effort into it. I'll never forget talking with some of the other people who were in there. They were talking about their slips, and I said, "You are all just weak-minded. You just have to make your mind up that you aren't going to do it, and don't do it anymore." In the meantime, however, I would leave my meeting and go get drunk!

I really didn't see myself as one of them. I hadn't lost much yet, and

I didn't see that alcohol or other drugs were the problem. I thought I was just having a run of bad luck. Getting high wasn't fun anymore; now I was just chasing the feeling of the first time I got high. I was looking for the time when I could control my using. I was searching for balance again. I had become so paranoid, and the more I used, the worse I got and the more I tried to control it. I was in competition with myself. I was determined to beat it.

After spending only a few weeks in that program, I found a doctor who tried to help me. We would meet and talk twice a week. I got deceptive, though, and these sessions became little more than a way to play games. He was doing the best he could, but I was not very receptive. I was in heavy denial.

This doctor then suggested I go to a center in Pennsylvania that ran a six-week transition program for people coming out of prison. They did have a good treatment program, but I had a very bad attitude. I viewed my time there as a vacation; I thought I could hang out, watch some TV, swim a bit, and a few weeks later I would come out fixed. They tried to help me, but at the same time they treated me like a famous ballplayer. I was getting special treatment just like I had all my life. I stayed there thirty-five days, never got honest, and never shared any emotions. I thought that just because I'd stopped doing drugs, I was better.

I still had no idea whatsoever what it was going to take for me to beat this thing. When I came back, I started calling the guys I used with just to see what was going on. I was still sick. I was just in the early stages of addiction. Like everything else in my life, I saw this as a win-lose situation. I hadn't yet been able to find a way to win, so I think subconsciously I was looking for a way to lose.

I got through the summer, worked out, and got in shape again. I was going to try to have the best year I could possibly have — just on willpower alone. Well, I wasn't back with the Bullets more that a couple days before I got high again! So much for willpower. I went to great lengths to hide what I was doing, but I couldn't. It was the same old story. Missing practices. Late for games. Thirty-five games into the 1982-83 season, I was suspended. I had a good contract there, but I blew it. They cut me, and now I was out of basketball. My coach didn't believe me anymore, and they finally said enough was enough.

Since I was out of basketball for the rest of that season, I decided I would go back into pro tennis — even though I hadn't played for three or four years. I worked on my game for about two months, and then started to play some tournaments — nothing major, just wild-card placements.

I pursued this tennis deal for a while, and then that summer another NBA possibility surfaced through Tom Nissalke again. Tom, who was now coaching the Cavaliers, signed me to a trial contract. I played in a summer league in California and I did well, even though I was still using drugs. There was a lot of pain for me, though, because I knew something was wrong. I hoped it was some other type of illness, that there was something else wrong with me. I just didn't want to believe that I was addicted to drugs. That possibility seemed terribly hopeless because I didn't know anyone who had ever stopped using. I'd never seen recovery.

Tom Nissalke

I wanted John in Cleveland, and I wanted to give him a chance to come back, too. I felt he could still play. He came to every practice, and he was terrific in the summer league.

I asked my son to hang around with John for a week just to see how John was doing, who his friends were, and so on. John was his usual energetic self. His schedule ran my seventeen-year-old son into the ground! He came back after a few days and said to me, "Dad, I have breakfast with him about 6:00 A.M., and then we go back to the room and watch a little TV. Then we go practice. We always practice basketball early. Come back, eat, and then it's tennis. We go out and play tennis for two to three hours, and then come back for more practice or a night game." To this day, my son still can't figure out how John could keep up that kind of pace.

I knew John had already been in rehab once or twice, but I didn't care about that. I wanted to sign John badly, both for his basketball and because I thought maybe I could help him out some. We'd always had really good rapport, and I felt we could talk about anything. Unbeknownst to me, my general manager already had his own guy picked out, so we didn't do it. That was the second incident I had with John that just crushed me.

I heard rumors that two of the owners of the Cavaliers got to talking about me and decided there were other guys around who could play for them who wouldn't be as risky as me, so they cut me before camp even started. Looking back, this may actually have been a blessing in disguise. There were guys on their team who were heavy drug users, so you can imagine what I'd have managed to do in *that* situation!

After the cut by the Cavaliers, I had run out of options in pro basketball. No one would let me come to a camp. Nobody thought I could play. My only other choice was semi-pro ball, and I decided I'd sign to play with the Lancaster Lightning in the Continental Basketball League (CBA). In just over six years, I'd gone from being the number-one pick in the draft, the best in the game at his position (with a great contract!), to living just this side of minimum wage. The CBA was an eternity from the chartered plane—major hotel life of the NBA. We're talking sixteen-hour bus rides every day with the players doing the driving.

We'd gone through a couple weeks of training camp and were one game into the season when I called Bob Bass in San Antonio and said, "B. B., you've got to help me! You've got to get me out of here!" I was desperate. I just couldn't take it. I also knew the Spurs needed a guard. They knew about me, too, and they felt anybody who had fallen from where I had been and was willing to go to the CBA must be serious about playing. And I was! So Bass let me come into San Antonio to show what I could do. They put me in a game. I scored fifteen points and really played well, and on December 13, 1983, they signed me.

I was always able to maintain my basketball skills despite my drug use because I worked out doubly hard to stay in shape. In the twisted way I was thinking then, I felt that by using, I was giving other people a chance to be equal. By being up all night drugging, I felt I was evening the tables. It gave me another goal to strive for — to see how messed up I could get myself and still have a good game.

I never wanted to be just a regular drug addict, I wanted to be the best. Whatever amount of drugs we did, I had to make sure I was still standing when we finished. My ego was running rampant, and I still didn't have any idea what an addiction was.

Bob Bass

In early December of 1983, we needed a point guard. I'd kept tabs on Luke and knew he was playing up in the CBA. I also knew that almost everybody else in the league was staying away from him because of his problems.

I can't even remember the city I went to, but I know I got up at 5:00 A.M. to fly to Boston. I rented a car and drove off somewhere down in Massachusetts where they were playing this CBA game. It was cold and snowing. It was a hell of a trip for a guy from Texas.

I went in there to see Luke play, to talk to him, to see how he was. Naturally he played well, and after the game was over, he literally got down on his knees, looked up at me, and said, "Please, B. B., please get me out of the back of this station wagon." They had driven all night to get to this place. Now, after the game, they were going to get back in the car and drive somewhere else. That's what it's like in the CBA.

We sent him a plane ticket, flew him into San Antonio, and signed him to a contract. We felt it was worth the risk to sign him. I talked to his agent, David Falk, a long time, and we decided he deserved another chance.

John played very well for us that year. He could still run a team. We won more than we lost, but we weren't a great team in spite of having a couple big-time scorers in George Gervin and Mike Mitchell.

John could really create a shot for other people. He

could penetrate well, he pushed it up on the break, and he was an excellent passer. I remember in Indiana one night. He must have had thirty points. John and Mike Mitchell went out on a scoring binge. We were isolating John at the top of the key. He was just unstoppable. Another night, George Gervin made one of his famous finger rolls, and John walked out from the bench onto the floor to high-five Gervin as he was going to the free throw line. The referee gave John a technical for six men on the floor. John should never complain about players like Dennis Rodman, given some of the stuff he's done on the court!

I think his strong point was that he was just a great competitor who could make a big shot at the end of the game. We were playing Chicago one night, and we had this play where we cleared a side for him and he drove from the top of the key and hit a left-handed running hook to win the game in overtime. I remember another game with Detroit where he hit a big three-pointer against Detroit from the right corner to win us that game.

More than anything, John always had a feel for the game — it's a special gift. Some guys who are very good basketball players don't really know how to play — their athleticism lets them get the job done. John had both gifts. He could shoot the ball from three-point range, he could penetrate and get inside the defense and score, or he could kick it off to people. He knew who his best players were, and he'd get the ball to them in a position where they could do something with it.

That ticket to San Antonio was one of the most beautiful plane tickets I'd ever seen. I couldn't wait to get there. We had a good team with George Gervin, Artis Gilmore, Mike Mitchell, Johnny Moore, John Paxton, Fred Roberts, Edgar Jones, and others. We didn't do great, but I averaged ten points and ten assists for the season, the first time in my career I averaged a double-double.

I was still drinking and I did some coke, but I didn't miss any practices or games. Everybody thought that the San Antonio area was the best place for me, because I didn't have any problems that year. I really liked Bob Bass; actually, I really liked the whole organization.

I played so well that I went into the free agent market following my season with the Spurs. The Rockets already had Hakeem Olajuwon and Ralph Sampson, and they were looking for a point guard. They offered me a contract for more than the Spurs wanted to pay, so I signed with Houston and the Spurs got some compensation. I went back to Houston and I got myself in trouble again. Actually, I was starting to get bad again in the summer. And before our first preseason game with San Antonio, before the trade, I missed a practice because I was doing drugs. I didn't know it then, but I was now finally heading toward the bottom.

Debbie Lucas

While we were in San Antonio, John was still having problems. He made his practices and games, sure, but he wasn't clean. The children — John, Jr., and Tarvia — knew something was going on. If you live in a house with an addict, it affects the whole family. The kids couldn't say what was going on with John, but they knew something was happening. They seemed to feel a need to protect him. John-John would get in the bed with John and just wrap his arms around him, like he knew his daddy needed to be held or something.

Both kids were in a Christian school and were getting a real solid Christian upbringing. When I would get mad at John, Tarvia would say, "Dad will be all right, Mom. Dad will be all right. God's watching him." One time when she was only in second grade, she told her dad that he would be held liable for her because she was a gift of God.

I was upset with John because things were getting worse, but I never said negative things about him to the kids. I don't believe your kids should be pulled into these kind of problems, or that one parent should try to make the kids turn against the other parent.

I tried to have a good home life for them and do special things. John wasn't using all the time, but the kids did see some of it. They cried for him when he didn't come home, or they'd grab onto him when he was going out, telling him to stay home. I think they felt that they needed to protect him. When he came back, they would run to get him things — sodas and the like — to make him feel special.

I went back to Durham for a while after finishing the season in San Antonio, and that's when my mother really came to the forefront. She was at home all day and knew when stuff was going on. My parents never saw my drugs, but they knew something was wrong. She'd wait up every night for me to come home. She would write down the license numbers of the cars that came to pick me up or drop me off, and then give them to the police.

My sister, Cheryl, was watching all this happen, too, and she was very angry. She'd seen me accomplish a lot in my short life, and now, when she saw it all slipping away, she felt betrayed and let down. We all began to have spiritual conversations. My mother would try to get me to read spiritual things and go to church. I even joined, thinking that it might help. Through all that pain, I began to see and feel the really unconditional love between us. My mother's spirituality and her love for her son and my sister's love really brought our immediate family much closer. I described our love before as *respect* love, but now, because of my addiction, it became more *unconditional* love. It was there despite all that was going on.

Cheryl Lucas

I had been with John and some of his friends a few years earlier when everyone was using so much. But once I realized he was going out of control, I stepped away from those peo-

ple. I thought that as his sister, as someone who really loved him, I could set an example or be a warning to make him change. He really respected my views and ideas, and he had always listened to my advice in the past. I told him I thought the situation had gotten out of hand, that he had to quit. But it was something that he never gave up; instead he just kept going further and further out there.

By now, using had really changed him a lot. He was thin. He was up most of the time. A couple of times I physically fought him. One night, I threw flower pots at him. I had just really had it. I had come home from work to see all of this cocaine on my kitchen table. I screamed at John and his friends, "What is going on? Whose stuff is this? Don't you know we could all be arrested for this? How can you let your group of friends bring this stuff in the house?"

Then I threw everything off the table and onto the floor. What I didn't throw on the floor, I flushed down the toilet. You should have seen how everybody's face froze. We're talking three to four thousand dollars worth of cocaine!

I just did whatever I felt I had to do to try to show him what was happening to him. But what I failed to realized was that no matter what I did, it was John who had to decide. It took me a while to understand that no matter how much you love a person, their life is still their life and you can't control it. Only they can. But I just wondered when he was going to wake up and see what he was doing to his life. What he was doing to himself was like painting a diamond. Given all the ability and talent that he had, to just see him walking around in that state was really disheartening to everybody. We all were always wishing we had one iota of the talent he had because we knew what we would do with it. But here's this person acting like it's not important to him.

Yet through all of this John never changed his basic personality. He might not show up for something, but when you were around him, he was the same guy. It was almost like he *had a guardian angel on his shoulder, too. I mean he never got shot. He never got beat up. He never overdosed.*

I'm a pretty spiritual person and I would pray 24 hours a day, 7 days a week, 365 days a year. We all just kept loving and supporting him through this. Obviously he wasn't doing exactly what we wanted him to do, but we didn't love him any less for it.

Nobody could understand why I was using drugs so much, why I was addicted to alcohol and cocaine. People would say, "Now, wait a minute, he doesn't have the characteristics of a drug addict." They saw a guy from a loving family, a guy with a good education, a guy who was one of the best in not just one sport but two, a guy who had money, fame, a loving wife and kids.

Those are all the outside parts. What wasn't so easy to see was my inside — what I was feeling, what was driving me. In a sense, I was an addict from the age of ten, and by this I mean I always had a powerful single-minded focus. I was hooked on success. I was hooked on competition. I was hooked on being the best, on winning at all costs, and I was hooked on love.

Yes, on love — the adulation and love of others. I love being around a lot of people even today. I got a lot of accolades, recognition, friends, and attention from being in sports. Take a basketball game — that's an event in front of a lot of people. You're out there and when you do well, people jump and scream, they want to be around you after the game, you make them happy. Then look what happens when you go to the library to study for a stupid history test, and then get a good grade!

By growing up in sports, I'd become a very one-sided person. I know what I was doing when it came to sports, but not in the other parts of life. Take emotions as an example. I never grew up emotionally because I didn't have to. Sports was a very safe, sheltered environment — through college, anyway. I received accolades and praise, and everything was taken care of for me. I never had to struggle with any difficulties or failures. And the rare times when strong and painful emotions came up, I used drugs to medicate the pain away. Sports was the necessity in my life, education an aside. I never *had* to use my education, I never had to develop a life outside sports, so I didn't.

With talent and some hard work, basketball came to me at all levels. But by the time I was two or three years into the pros, I found myself without another level to go to, without any other challenges. Then basketball became a job to me. I'd always lived for the next level, so I tried to find other ways to motivate myself — and one great possibility for doing that, one that never occurred to me, was my education. I not only had my degree, but I had gone on to graduate school while I was playing at Golden State and earned a master's degree in education administration. But I just let it all sit.

There are some things people need to understand about the professional sports life. It *is* just a job — a very well paid one with some great opportunities — but still a job. People think that playing and coaching and flying all over the country is just great, but that's bull. All they see is the game and the glamour. Any pro player will tell you that the glamour wears off after the first time around the league, after you play against all the guys you've seen on TV. Now you say, "Jesus, this is a job."

In the pros, the game changes to what people don't see. The practice this morning. Getting on that plane at 11:30 or midnight after the game, arriving at your hotel at 2:00 or 3:00 A.M., and needing to be up for practice and sometimes even a game the next day. Waking up wondering what city you're in. And then the coaches and the fans expecting you to perform like you should every night — because you make all that money. The charter flights we have now make everything a little more convenient, but they don't really change much. The days are still hectic, and like everyone else, you're working. Most people don't know what it's like to come down to a restaurant to eat some breakfast and all of the sudden, there's a crowd around you who think you'd just love to sign autographs. Everywhere you go, they're there. If you're a star like David Robinson, or Dennis Rodman, or Michael Jordan, you can't go anywhere in public with any privacy. Yet despite all the crowds and publicity, it's a lonely life. I mean *real* lonely. You're away from family and friends a lot.

And there are all the things that your parents told you that you have to look out for. People never see this in sports, but it's there. You have to look out because this is business. Guys mad at you because you make more money than they do. Bargaining with owners. Sudden trades that uproot you from teammates, friends, and even family. People always looking for something from you, wanting to be your agent, to be a financial partner in this and that. There are women, sex, drugs. It's all there, waiting to take you down.

Next, there's the eighty-two-game season. In college, the season was just long enough at twenty-five to twenty-seven games to keep the hunger to play there without it being too much. But in the pros, you play eighty-two games. My God, that's a lifetime! And then the playoff season starts.

High school and college ball is great. "Let's win one for the home team!" Everybody in the bus together going to and from games, cheerleaders there, too. Crowds of people you know, people you see every day at school. It's an exciting time. But suddenly you get to the pros and the roar of the crowd disappears. Where are the guys? Where are the cheerleaders? It's like having cold water thrown on you.

I didn't know how to cope with it. All I had learned about how to live, I had learned from sports. I was still using the principles of athletics to live by; I didn't understand or have the principles of daily life or love. I was always looking and searching for something better. I didn't know when good was good enough. I was searching for that spirit my parents had when they went to church. I found it in alcohol and cocaine. Drugs made me feel that wonderful wholeness that I wanted so badly to feel. Drugs made me feel connected and happy. But they were destroying my life and career, too. I was in a lot of pain, I was starting to have some bad losses, but I still didn't see what drugs were doing to me and the others in my life. I still didn't know that all along I was using drugs to fill a big hole inside me.

CHAPTER 6

⊚

RECOVERY

From October 1984, when the Spurs traded me to Houston, to March 1986, when I was kicked off the team, I finally bottomed out from drug use. Willpower didn't work. Half-hearted attempts at treatment didn't work. Counsel and cautions from family, friends, teammates, and coaches were equally worthless.

It was after that blackout in Houston and when I'd tested positive after lying to my coach and in front of thousands of fans that I returned to Van Nuys for my second and last attempt at treatment there. I was sick and tired of living the way I was. I was in so much pain by then, I didn't care if I ever played basketball again. I just wanted drugs out of my life. I wanted to be free so badly. I told my counselors, "I am ready to do whatever you tell me to do."

I mean, I was *desperate*. I was *ready*, and this time I listened. At first I really didn't much know what I was doing there. I wasn't thinking about anything, analyzing everything like I'd done before. I just surrendered. I was willing to do *anything* to get free of drugs.

In each of my previous trips into treatment, I went alone. This time was different. I asked my parents, Debbie, and my kids to join me. This time I wanted them to be part of it. I knew they had to for me to get better. This was a very emotional time for me — and for them, too — and it was the toughest thing I'd ever done. I had violated all my values while I was addicted, and I needed to reestablish them. I decided to put the Twelve Step principles into my life. I wanted to start developing my character again. I had to do it with my family, and with their help.

Blond Lucas

When we arrived at Van Nuys to be with John, one of the first things that came out was how very worried John was about how we felt about him, his drug problems, and his going into treatment. We told him straight out that we would do anything to help — we'd be there for him, go to counseling with him, whatever. Our going to Van Nuys convinced John that we truly were behind him.

Besides having to face some very strong emotions, another thing that made treatment so hard was that I finally I got honest. Real honest. I had to admit to everybody what I'd been doing. I had to admit that Debbie wasn't the problem, that the kids weren't the problem, that my parents weren't the problem, that basketball wasn't the problem. The problem was me. I told them that I knew I had to sort out every part of my life.

One of the first things I did was have a real straight talk with my parents. All my life I'd been trying to please them, especially my dad. He had always meant a lot to me. I looked up to him so much that I had made him into God for me. I remember a time when my dad and uncle wrestled. They called my uncle Big Ben because he was about 6' 9" and 295 pounds. Now my dad is about 5' 10" — not a big fellow, but on the first go round, my dad got Uncle Ben's leg and twisted it around and pinned him. I was really impressed. Uncle Ben's son insisted that they wrestle again because he was upset that his dad had lost. I don't think my dad wanted to do it again because he knew he was lucky the first time — and that my uncle had really just let him win. In the next round, since Ben's son had been so disappointed, Ben simply picked my dad up and held him over his head.

I couldn't believe my eyes. I was crushed. I lay awake all night worrying. That was my first realization that my dad wasn't the best at everything. It really bothered me, but then I tried to reconcile the loss by saying my dad was still really good. I kept asking him, "Dad, you let him do that, didn't you? You let him win, didn't you?" I just couldn't believe he wasn't the greatest, and I kept that attitude into my adult life.

A turning point in treatment came for both my dad and me when we were talking to the counselors. He told me that he had always worshipped me. If something didn't go my way on the court, he would say that it just couldn't be my fault; someone else missed a play. Or if I shot a ball at the end of a game and it didn't go in, he'd say to himself that there must be something wrong with the goal. He couldn't accept my failures, just as I had realized for the first time that I couldn't accept his failures, either.

I'll never forget that day. I told him, "Dad, you can't be God in my life any longer. It's too hard for me, it causes me too much trouble. I've been striving and striving to be just like you. I have to stop trying to make you proud of me." I realized I had to start living my life for *me.*

There were thirty people in that group, including my whole family. It was so hard to talk — me and my dad sitting there in front of everybody. I started crying and then he started, too. And do you know what he said to me then? He said, "Son, I guess you can't be God in my life, either." At last we finally realized we could look at each other as human beings. We told each other that we could love each other even if we weren't perfect.

I talked to my mother, too. I told her I wanted to change, that I loved her. I thanked her for caring for me, even when I didn't care for me. She said, "Son, I just want you to be happy."

In another group session, I told Debbie I hadn't been the best husband. She said she knew that. And I talked to my kids. I had two kids then: Tarvia, who was seven, and John, Jr., who was three. I felt so, so bad for what I had put my children through. I couldn't see what I was doing at the time, but it was so obvious to me now. I used to do drugs in my house, and both the kids would imitate me. Tarvia used to take ashes out of the ashtray and put them up on her nose like she'd seen me do with cocaine. And she would act paranoid just like I used to — running from window to window, looking out to see if anyone was coming up to the house. And John used to put a bunch of bottles of water in his gym bag before he'd go out. I asked him once what the heck he was doing, and he said, "I got to get my beer like you, got to get my brews." It was just heartbreaking. I told them I would be a better father for them, and that I was sorry for how I'd been.

Bringing all of us together also helped us as a family to clear the air. There was some friction between Debbie and my parents, friction that I was at the root of because I'd been playing them against each other — telling my parents that Debbie was the problem, and vice-versa. It's natural that there were some hard feelings between them. No one was really ugly to one another, but my troubles just caused a tension among everyone involved. My parents didn't know all that was really happening for a long time. For the first few years of my addiction, I was the perfect son when I went home.

Once I got to the core and admitted the problem, I was sorry. I felt that I had embarrassed everyone, and I was very concerned about what I was doing to them. After this stuff was all out on the table, my father said to me, "This is good what we're doing here, but talk isn't enough. I don't want any more lip service. Now you got to do it."

Blond Lucas

Up until Van Nuys, John had lied to all of us about what was going on. Now John has always been taught by both of us to tell the truth. We had told him all during the years we were raising him, "Whatever you get into, tell the truth. Once you don't have to lie anymore, you're free." We taught the kids in our schools the same lesson. I would say to them, "Tell me the truth the first time and we won't have to go through a whole lot of trouble later." We used to talk a lot, that the best things in life are those things that are free — love, honesty, integrity, friendship, being able to sleep at night with a clear conscience.

But yes, John had lied to us. He told us there was nothing wrong. Once I even asked him if he was sick, and he said, "No, Mom, just don't worry. I'm going to straighten myself out."

When John finally told the truth there at Van Nuys, I could have shouted. It was strengthening to his father and me when he did that. We felt that at least he had carried something over from his childhood that we had tried to teach him. Even though it hurt to hear it all, there was something good in his demonstrating that he could tell the truth. And once the truth was out, it was freeing for him — just like we always told him.

John Lucas, Sr.

When we first found out about John's drug use, we went through a period of wondering where we had gone wrong. How is it that he could do drugs and be around us so much and without our knowing about it? And then we thought we were the only parents with this problem. We were that naive. But the more you listen, the more you learn. We weren't the only ones with this problem. We came to the conclusion that many other children from all walks of life have this problem, too. Why should we feel that our child necessarily had to be exempt. Why couldn't it just as well happen to John as someone else?

Blond and I never reached the point of blaming each other for this. We always saw it as our problem. We never said, "Does anybody on your side of the family have this? Was your daddy or cousin a drunk?" We never did that; we accepted it for what it was. Once we found out what was happening, we didn't condemn him, but we didn't try to hide the truth either. We told people what was what. We had always lived like that, and we couldn't see a reason to change over this.

Blond Lucas

I prayed every kind of prayer you could possibly pray. I was asking for different things and they weren't coming. So one night when we heard on TV that John had missed a plane or something, I said, "Lord I don't know what to ask for anymore, but I tell you this. Just let Your will be done and give me strength to accept it." That's the very last prayer I ever prayed. I had been asking Him to straighten out John, to do this or to do the other. Those prayers don't work. You have to let Him do His own work.

Lucas and I found that we could appreciate each other and love each other in trials as well as in success. And that's what we see this as — a trial, not a failure. Adversity can bring families closer together rather than causing you to give up. Even after the darkness of night, there's still a sunrise to be seen. We told each other that it could be worse. It could have been anything. John could have died.

John Lucas, Sr.

Blond's word — trial — is perfect. I think before all of this happened, I would have called John's experience a failure — his and ours. I think I could have told you what failure was, too, but now I'm not so sure that I can. I really believe this was adversity. It was a period in which we could see what we're each made of. Before this, we had been close, but never challenged particularly strongly. Then when the bottom fell out and we felt that we couldn't make it, we didn't give up. We had enough to see it through. As John began his recovery, we began to feel that through these troubles John had actually brought us a deeper understanding and awareness of what love really is. Our family began to move to a new level of unconditional love. It's helped both John and us know and understand that there's something beyond us that guides our destinies. We can now appreciate the experiences we've had

— even though we may not have chosen them. Now that I've lived through it, however, I can say it was worth it.

I spent nearly two months as an inpatient at the treatment center at Van Nuys. I had a really difficult time at first, but then I saw a lot of big changes in me. I learned so much about myself, about who I was, how I saw myself, why I was doing what I was doing, and what was important to me. It was a crash course in becoming an adult.

I got so much help from the other people there, too, other recovering addicts. A fellow named Jack B. kept telling me something that I'd never realized before: that basketball is what I do, it's not who I am. He'd say, "John, we're *all* on a search to find out who we are." And someone else told me one day that I wasn't a bad person, I was just making some bad choices. That really made a difference for me.

By this time I was beginning to feel better. I was stronger. I could sleep better. But then I started having all these emotions. I didn't like feeling that much — feeling those moods. A lot of things had happened to me that I never let myself feel. The pain of Coach Easterling's death. Of my grandmother's death. Loneliness. I never let myself really feel the pain of living or losing. I was also learning how to do something without being certain of the outcome. That was *so* hard, too. I was always dying to know what the future would bring.

Not long before I went into Van Nuys this time, I met a guy who truly helped me get sober. His name was Cozy, and he was a striptease dancer in Houston. He would come to the games in Houston, walk down by the bench and ask me how I was doing. He looked like Prince, wearing purple all the time. I was always so scared to have him around me because everybody was laughing at me, saying, "Who's that guy, Lucas?" I'd tell him, "Go away, go away, man. I don't want you around me." Now here was a guy that fit my idea of an addict, but he was recovering. He knew I was relapsing all the time, and he kept calling on me to go back into treatment. That's when I began to learn that you have to drop all your prejudices to be in recovery.

I never thought that I could be an addict or alcoholic. I thought an alcoholic was a guy who lived on the park bench. I had the misconception that if you could afford to buy your drugs, you didn't have a drug problem — that you became addicted when you couldn't afford it. At Van Nuys, I kept looking for people who were different than me — but they were all just like me. Regular people. They didn't look like winos or junkies.

Through my years of addiction, I had managed to stay in really good physical condition. The treatment program I was in had a very strong clinical component, but there was nothing formal going on for physical conditioning — even though they had a great set of Nautilus equipment in the place. All this equipment was just sitting there unused. I really felt like I had to work my body, too, so I set up a conditioning program for myself.

I began to see exercise as medicine. Then one day, I got the idea for a fitness program — an anaerobic and aerobic workout program — for everyone in treatment. I began working on the idea while I was still in treatment. I dug up a pile of data on exercise and treatment. I developed an assessment tool, and then we tested it on patients who wanted to participate.

We discovered that everybody who was assessed came out "poor" on the scale — even after they'd been working out some. For example, maybe a guy could do ten pushups in his first attempt and twenty a week later, but twenty was still bad. By using the norms of the American College of Sports Medicine, the patients couldn't see any improvement. I wanted something for us that was going to build our self-esteem, so I took three years worth of data and developed my own norms for the assessment. Participants would take a preassessment when they first came into treatment, and then a post-assessment before they left. Finally people could be judged against other addicts and alcoholics rather than against norms based on the general population. If you improved, you got credit for it.

We started people on real exercise instead of the bingo or Ping-Pong they'd been doing, for two reasons. First, it's just plain good for your body and mind to be in decent condition. Second, the results of exercise can be seen and felt — they're very tangible — and you can get results quickly. People can see that they're helping their bodies more easily and sooner than they can see that they are helping their minds. People realize quickly that they can help themselves. It's a quick and effective way to boost self-esteem.

Through our work, we also discovered that many people would come into treatment fifteen pounds underweight and leave fifteen pounds overweight — a fluctuation of thirty pounds in thirty days. Now you've got another problem, you're too fat. Teaching exercise during treatment was not only a way to minimize that weight swing, it was a way to show people how to make it part of their everyday living. Once we had this program going, I began to develop a fitness book based on the principles of the Twelve Steps.

I came back to Houston after treatment not knowing what I as going to do to make a living. I was spending some time writing a booklet that outlined the whole program, and I was doing more research on fitness programs. I was also watching the Rockets go to the finals, staying sober, and collecting my monthly sobriety pins.

I had to come up with some new way to make a living because I thought I was out of basketball for good — that it wasn't my territory anymore. Bill Fitch had really put me down in the press. Robert Reed and some of the other players said that they didn't have pity for me, they had prayers. Two other guys on my team said everybody doing drugs should be suspended. (And *they* were the very next year. They ended up in my treatment center!) I just kept thinking that I didn't want to play any more basketball.

I began thinking even more about this concept of fitness as a component of treatment. I realized that I had people following me around wanting to exercise. Then one day it hit me that this was something I could do, and I decided to put this fitness program together and see if I could get hospital-based treatment centers to buy into it. What had started as just a comfortable physical assessment was now a carefully laid-out, daily program designed to fit as a formal component of treatment.

The city of Houston has a lot of hospital and treatment programs. I went from one to the next, and everybody I spoke to thought it was a good idea. Nobody, however, would give it — or me — a chance, and

I guess that shouldn't have surprised me. I didn't know much at all about hospitals. I was a notorious sniffer with only sixty days of sobriety, and most hospitals told me they required a person to have at least a year or two of sobriety before they would hire them to work in chemical dependency. What could I say? Here was a high-profile guy who'd been on a real bad and real long losing streak, pushing a new program no one's had before. Why should they take a chance?

And speaking of chances, mine were fading fast because now I had only one more hospital to contact. As you can imagine, I was more than a little discouraged because I really believed in this idea and thought it could help a lot of people. I also had no doubt that I could run the program. I called to see the administrator, Joyce Bossett, and had to wait nearly two weeks before I could get a meeting with her.

Joyce Bossett, vice president for mental health services, Columbia/Hospital Corporation of America

It was midsummer of 1986, and I was attending a conference in Nashville when I received a phone call from my hospital in Houston. They said that a fellow named John Lucas came in with a guy who was working on our chemical dependency unit. John was looking for a facility that would take a chance on the fitness program he had developed when he was in treatment in Van Nuys.

My first question was, who is John Lucas? They explained that John was the guy who was suspended from the Rockets just the previous spring for drug use. That rang a bell for me. I remembered that I was watching the late news the night when they did an interview with John after he had been tested for drug use with the Rockets — a test that turned out to be positive. John had said to the sportscaster, "Oh, absolutely not; it won't be positive." I looked at him and I thought, "That kid is really in trouble." I just knew it would be positive, though I couldn't tell you how.

I set up a luncheon meeting for John with some of the

other administrators in our boardroom. We walked him around the facility first, and then we came in to eat and talk. John was dressed in a flashy pinstripe suit. He seemed very stiff and very nervous, a little like a wild fawn. He was clearly out of his element. John only picked at his food while we talked, and he had a way of being very expressive with his hands, which would fly all over the place as he spoke. After the meeting, someone wondered if he wasn't still high because of his mannerisms and behavior, but I said, "Look, his idea may make sense. Let's reserve judgment and just hear this guy out."

When I finally met with John personally, he brought in a massive contract. He was all prepared to negotiate on this fitness program. I said, "John, take this back. You're not signing up to play for an NBA team, okay? If we do this, it will be part of our other treatment program."

I didn't exactly know that besides a job, I was also looking for aftercare. I did know that I had been through treatment like a shopper through a department store the day before Christmas. I had not been able to stay sober in the past, and something was missing. I was looking for that something.

Joyce said to me, "I'm interested in taking a chance on you, but you know you're a high risk. If you go down, I go down. I'm going to keep an eye on you and you're going to be monitored well, so if you want to do business with me, here's the deal."

We went first to meet Dr. James Considine. She told him, "Here's somebody I want you to put into therapy. I want you to see him every day. Don't charge him anything; we'll make him pay back later by giving back to somebody else. Get him into our aftercare program and into some groups, too."

Then Joyce told me that they would test me randomly. My first reaction was to say, "Hold it! You can't do that," but Joyce wouldn't budge. She said, "That's part of the deal. See the doctor, go to meetings, go to aftercare, and get tested. I'm going to be able to say that John Lucas is sober today. I'm not going to let this thing come up and bite me. That's the deal. Do you want it?"

I took a deep breath, danced around a bit, and then I said, "Yeah, fine. Let's go." Here was my chance at last.

Joyce Bossett

The next task I had was to deal with the internal politics. Here I was proposing to bring a total stranger into the hospital setting — a professional basketball player no less. I was being asked, "How on earth did he get into the health care field? Can he possibly do the job?" — that kind of thing. My reply was simply to say, "Aren't we in the business of helping people? Yes, of course we are. And here's a recovering addict, so let's help him. Let's put all the pettiness aside and see what we can do."

John immediately brought a positive energy to the hospital that you wouldn't believe, and staff began to rally behind him and his program. It took off internally, and soon other facilities began to call for information — and to talk with John to see if the program would work for them.

It's difficult to describe how much the opportunity to work at Joyce's hospital meant to me. It gave me a home for my recovery, and this was important to me — it was critical. I came to the hospital every day, I went to Twelve Step meetings, and I began to do things that really helped me. I was growing up. I was beginning, for the first time in my life, to have a life outside of sports. And at the same time, I began to feel that I had a home again. I was part of a team that was working together for a common goal. *That* I could understand.

Over the next few months, I just threw myself into my work — and into supporting my recovery. The program was catching on, not only at Houston International Hospital, but with others. I began to see how important it was to give back to others, too. If, for example, an individual finished treatment and needed a job — or longer aftercare — I would hire him or her to work as a fitness technician alongside the exercise physiologist for ninety days. That would in turn help him or her stay in recovery. And when I got my first fitness program up and running, one of the first hired was Cozy. I did that because he was there for me when nobody else was — not even the guys who were supposed to be my friends and my teammates.

It wasn't very long before we all began to realize that the program was becoming quite successful. Once it had been a component of the hospital's chemical dependency treatment program for a while, we began getting many inquiries from other centers and hospitals. The professionals in the field began to see the therapeutic benefit for their patients. I was on my way, and eventually this program became the first component of John H. Lucas Enterprises.

What I began to learn from Joyce and the others at the hospital went beyond the knowledge of running a fitness program. When I entered treatment at Van Nuys that second time, my adult world was little more than an extension of my high school basketball world. At the hospital, I was at last getting the kind of experiences that a lot of people get much sooner in life — in their teens and early twenties — as they ease their way into the adult world. I was doing stuff that to them seems commonplace — participating in planning meetings, speaking to the public, making sales calls, and so on. But to me they were all new and scary. Joyce and the other staff were helping me become an adult in the adult world.

Joyce Bossett

I certainly don't mean this in a demeaning way, but initially, working with John was a little like raising a child. I was very domestic and maternal. At one point, for example, after John had been with us for four or five months, he was invited to speak in front of a huge kids' rally at the Astrodome in Houston. When I heard about the invitation, I said, "Have John

Lucas come into my office. I need to talk to him and I don't want anybody around."

John came in, saw me, and got the expression on his face he often had when I talked to him — like I was the Wicked Witch of the West. He said, "What did I do now?" "Nothing," I said. "I just want to talk to you."

John was standing nervously, wearing the old-style basketball shorts — not the longer baggy style popular today. I said, "You have to put your warm-ups on whenever you come to the administrative offices and in every unit you go to. You have to dress the part; this is a different ball game you're playing now."

Then I asked him to take a seat right in front of me. I pulled a chair up and told him I wanted him to sit on his hands. He looked at me like I was crazy, so I said, "Okay, just give me your hands for now. Put them in mine, and talk to me about what you'll say at this event."

As John spoke, his hands pulled and tugged at mine, trying to fly this way and that. I asked, "Do you see what you're doing?" He didn't, and so I said, "John, if you go out to speak in front of a big audience with your hands flying around like this, I guarantee you the press will say you're drunk. That's my point, that's why I want you to sit on your hands."

John did sit on his hands, and I made him talk to me for five minutes about what he was planning to say. Well, John moved that chair all over that room, but his hands stayed put. John finally began to really understand that he was going to be on stage, and that meant he had to think about how he was presenting himself. I'd been telling him for a while that he was a public figure, that he'd probably be one for a long time to come, that he would have to work his recovery on stage, and it would be hard work. "People will judge you," I said. "They'll speculate about you, and you have to know you're okay." I helped John work on his speech, and a week later he was at the Astrodome.

This was the first time I had ever spoken publicly. I was pretty nervous. It was right before basketball season was to start and they had all the media there — the same folks who'd covered my story when I had lied to the whole damn city about my test being negative. Well, I basically did a Fourth Step in that talk. I told those kids I hadn't been the best of fathers. I told them how my daughter had seen me snorting cocaine, how drugs had cost me my job and a lot of my career. I just told them about many of the things that had happened to me.

Joyce Bossett

I walked into John's speech and was standing in the back when he stood up to begin speaking. It was obvious to me that he was a bit nervous, but he came off like you wouldn't believe, and the kids asked him great questions. While he was talking, he seemed to be looking for someone, and I finally realized he was looking for me. He wanted to show me, I guess, that he was doing okay.

I had to laugh a bit because he was holding the podium on both sides, sort of walking it around the stage a bit because he was so active. He was simply mobbed by the kids afterwards. They wanted to talk to him and get his auto-graph. We literally had to pull him away from the place.

Afterward, John, a couple other folks from work, and I went to a coffee shop. We were critiquing the talk, and John had very little to say. I said, "John, please don't take this per-sonally — we all do this for one another after speeches to help us improve. It's the way we do business. If we're doing a deal and it goes sour, or if it goes well, we want to know why. We're going to look at what you did today and we're going to decide whether this was a success or not — and why."

We were discussing a few things he'd done well, when John just jumped up from the table and said, "I'm very sorry. I've just got to go to a meeting, I've got to go." And he was gone!

We all went back to the hospital after we finished talking, and about an hour later, he called. "I had to go to a meeting because I was on stage and I felt good. I was nervous but I felt good. I was beginning to feel that I was okay, and I got scared. I just had to go to a meeting and talk to folks to get this out." I told him that he'd done the right thing, and that I understood how he was feeling. I tried to let him know that he could and would begin to find success, and good feelings, from his new work — and that was okay.

By this time I had become entrenched in my recovery program and in sobriety. I went to a Twelve Step meeting every single day at 6:30 A.M. I felt I should do that *before* my day started, not in the evening after work. Meetings were my Higher Power, and I felt this was a very good way to start the day. Even when I was traveling for work, I would find a place in each town or city where I could attend a meeting. I would always go wearing my warm-ups, looking like a ballplayer. No one at the meetings knew who I was until one day I was on TV and a few people recognized me. The next day when I arrived at my meeting, the teasing began. They told me, in truth, that they thought those sweats and old sneakers were the only clothes I had. They had felt so sorry for me that they were actually getting a collection together to get me some better shoes and stuff!

I learned a lot from the people I met at meetings. And I still do. I still go to meetings all the time. I doubt that I've missed more than a dozen days since I've been sober. I want my sobriety, and meetings are like a lifeline to me.

Joyce Bossett

Just watching John grow was so rewarding. He really began to understand his sobriety and to value it. It seemed that when John went to his meetings during his first six or nine months of sobriety, he was kind of caught up in them as being a little exciting and different. I think he was holding back in those meetings, but eventually he began to truly hear other people's issues, and he began to understand that people really came to share and get support.

Remember, John was healing, too. He didn't have to focus so hard anymore on his own recovery. And once John understood this, he would listen carefully to what people said, and the next thing you knew he was trying to help somebody on the side. He was forever coming into Administration and saying, "Can you just give me a bed for a couple of days?" I would tell him, "John, this is not a county or city hospital, okay? I can't open up a Lucas wing for all of your stray buddies." But he kept pressing me, saying, "No, I'm telling you that some really great rewards will come out of helping these guys."

"Yeah," I said, "like a lot of bad debt."

One day he came into my office wanting to know exactly what I meant by "a lot of bad debt." I sat down with him and explained how a hospital is run. "There's a master budget for the hospital, and I'm responsible for the bottom line," I told him. "I'm supposed to deliver x amount of dollars at the end of every year." I suggested he equate that to a projected goal of how many tickets the Rockets would sell in a season, what they'd make in concessions, cable and TV rights, and so on. I said, "Their revenues come in through these different departments, and so does ours." I explained, too, how we project the number of patients that we'll have, Medicare payments, contracts with HMOs — the whole business. John took the information and he dissected it. A few days later we got back together and he was talking bad debt and asking how many patients we could put in free beds. I explained how that depended on the day's census and the patient mix. He figured it all out, and the next thing I knew, he showed up in my office saying, "Well, I think we have one opening, and I've got someone who can use it."

I tell you, John didn't just learn the business, he mastered it. He has a mind like a steel trap. He probably could have run a facility by this point. John wanted to know everything, and once we discovered how much he did know, we began to pull him into some of our strategic planning sessions. He just walked all over everybody with his marketing knowledge. He could tell us what we should do, how we should do it, the contacts we should make. He was giving us names of people to contact. He was amazing. The folks in the marketing department couldn't believe it. He was a born marketer.

John was like a sponge — he watched every move I made and just absorbed it. It was like osmosis. Of course, he had an inflated opinion of my ability — still does, too! I remember one day telling him, "John, I think we're approaching the point where the student is overtaking the master." And he said, "Well, I want to be at least as good as the master." Then I asked him if he was competing with me, and he smiled and said, "Just a tad, I guess." Working with John was simply very rewarding.

Only six or seven months after I came out of that cocaine blackout on the streets of downtown Houston, I was deeply committed to an aftercare program in a hospital, and my drug tests (with *my* urine!) were consistently clean. I was working in a field that meant a lot to me, I'd created a program more and more hospitals were interested in, and I was earning an income. I was really beginning to get my principles in place, and I was growing a lot as a person and as a businessman. I had a life outside sports. I was on the unit every day, working with the guys, building up the treatment and aftercare components, and trying to do some marketing. It really helped my recovery to work with people like this who had less sobriety than me because it made me feel like I wasn't alone.

I had been telling Joyce that athletes really needed more help to get off drugs. We athletes needed more help understanding the disease concept of addiction because it was so foreign to us — we all tend to think it's just a lack of willpower and discipline. That's the sports approach to life again. And we needed better aftercare. Joyce agreed, and by the summer of 1986, not only were my fitness *and* aftercare programs in place, we had four or five professional athletes in treatment — including two guys who'd played with me in Houston and had gotten banned from the league. More and more teams and athletes were inquiring about the program because they finally knew an athlete who was staying sober. All the other guys kept slipping and getting banned from the NBA, but I was staying sober. Especially given my history, everybody wanted to know what I was doing right.

Then Lenny Bias, a graduate of the University of Maryland and the number-one pick of the Celtics, died of a cocaine overdose. Suddenly, cocaine is a big problem, drugs are a big problem, it's a major deal because now somebody had died. The drug issue was pole-vaulted up in front of everything. As sad as Lenny's death was, it had a positive effect. Now people who got caught using drugs began to get some compassion. No longer was drug use seen only as a moral issue; more and more people began to see it as a disease.

It's so curious how fate moves. Here I am working in this field, an addict in recovery, and suddenly the media and everyone wants to talk to *me* about drugs and treatment. I became a spokesman.

About eight months into my recovery, something else happened — I began to get feelers from some of the pro clubs wondering if I wanted to play pro ball again. Some teams were definitely interested in me. I thought about this a lot, and then called a press conference. I announced that while I had eight months of recovery and sobriety behind me and was doing great, I just didn't think I was ready to go back to basketball. By this time, my sobriety was more important to me than anything else, and I didn't want to jeopardize it by taking a chance on pro ball. Maybe sometime, I thought to myself, but not yet.

CHAPTER 7

RETURN TO BASKETBALL

It started in the fall of 1986. I had to admit to myself that basketball was calling me again. I was thinking about playing, and I'd go up to the hospital's gym and shoot whenever I could. One day, Joyce stopped in the gym and asked me if I wanted to go back. I told her I was going back. "I'm going back whenever I'm strong enough and I get an offer. It doesn't have to be a good offer, but I'm going back," I told her.

Not long after that conversation, I got a call from Del Harris, the assistant coach of the Milwaukee Bucks, telling me they were interested in signing me. I told him I still wasn't ready for basketball. I still wasn't certain I was ready to try it.

Joyce Bossett

In late November or early December, after John had talked again to Del Harris, I gave him a call. Del wanted to know if we could guarantee that John would stay sober. I said, "No, and he can't either. No one in the world can. But I can tell you that John has the tools he needs to help him stay sober." I told Del that we were going to design a system for John that will give him more support for his recovery when he was on the road. We would have a counselor from one of our hospi-

tals call him at every city he plays in. Then, when John got to his hotel, we'd have a number and a name for him — a counselor he could meet with. And we would tell him to call in to us every day — he could talk to a counselor, to Dr. Considine, or me — whoever he wanted. I said to Del, "John will not be without support. That we can promise."

The aftercare and counseling program Joyce and Dr. Considine set up for me became the model used for the NBA's own program just a few years later. I was the guinea pig. Nothing like this had been in place when I was struggling to maintain sobriety in previous seasons. I could have used it, but I probably wasn't ready to get sober then anyway.

By December 1986, I felt I was finally strong enough to go back to basketball. I called Del and asked him for a meeting. The day he was flying in, I was so excited. I was running around dressing in the hospital. Debbie had to bring my clothes over because I'd forgotten them when I left the house. Everyone was trying to help me. It was like they were getting their son ready for the prom. But then Debbie forgot my belt, so I had to go into the meeting holding up my pants — it was pretty funny. We had a good meeting, but I still didn't give them my okay. This was a huge decision for me, and I needed to think on it just a little longer.

A few weeks later, I went to talk to the Bucks' coach, Don Nelson. I was still hesitant, but he said to me, "John, if you can't make it here, you won't be able to make it anywhere. You'll have all the help you need. But I have to tell you, I'm not going to change my life just because you're on the team. This is Milwaukee, and I'm still going to drink my beer — and you're going to continue to live your own life." After that extra push from Don, I made my decision. I signed a contract and put myself back in pro ball again! On January 18, 1987, I played my first game with no practice except a shoot-around. I led the team in assists, and we came back from twenty points down to win.

I began to realize pretty quickly that playing basketball would give me a platform to carry the message of sobriety to athletes, fans, and

John on the road to the North Carolina State Tennis Championship.

With high school mentor, Coach Carl "Bear" Easterling.

Luke directs traffic as star point guard at the University of Maryland.

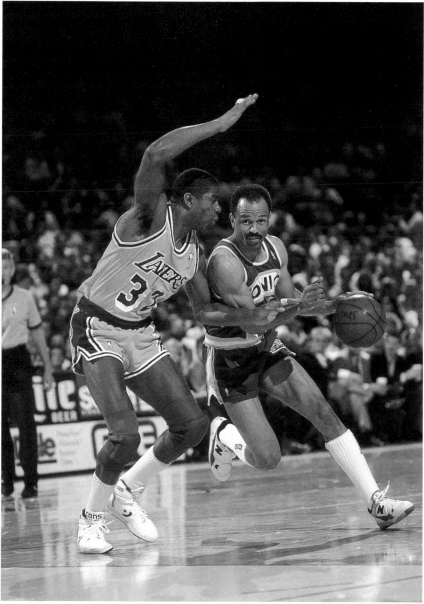

Photo by Andrew D. Bernstein

Luke drives on Magic.

Coaching the Spurs to the 1993 NBA playoffs.

John with his mom, Blondola; dad, John Sr.; and sister, Cheryl.

other people. I think I would have gotten a lot of exposure and media attention regardless, but I was getting even more because we were a winning team. People would come up behind the bench before the games and say Twelve Step slogans like, "Easy does it," or "One day at a time," just to let me know I wasn't alone. During the national anthem, I would see people in the crowd giving me a knowing look or nod. I don't think people really saw me as a basketball player anymore. I was someone who was *one of them*. Lots of people have had family members or somebody else they know who struggled through something very difficult in their lives. I was an example of someone who had, too, and was now making it.

You might think I was proud of this, but I really wasn't. In fact, I struggled with it. I was worried about what would happen if I didn't make it, if I relapsed. I didn't want to jeopardize the reputation of Twelve Step programs. If I slipped, I didn't want people pointing at me and saying, "See, they don't work." But my sponsors and other people I knew well said to me, "John, you may be the only part of recovery some people get to see. Don't worry about all that. Just do what you've been doing."

Now I was getting cheers again instead of boos. But not from everybody. I took a lot of shots, especially when I first came back. I'll never forget in Philadelphia one night, against the 76ers, I went to the line to shoot a free throw and some guys shouted down at me, "Hey, Lucas, don't snort that line." When we went to play in San Antonio, one of the TV announcers refused to call my name. He felt I shouldn't be in the league, so every time I would score, he would say, "Basket by J. L." In Sacramento, a guy stuck a sign on the back of my jersey that said "Things go better with coke." I didn't know it was there, and I walked out on the court with it. Another night in Portland against the Blazers, some guy sitting right behind the bench kept making snorting noises. I just turned to him and said, "God loves you, and I love you too."

I had to go through a lot of that, and believe me, there was a lot of pain. But I didn't care. I finally knew what I was. I was an addict and an alcoholic, and as long as it didn't bother me, I didn't care what anyone else said. This was the first time in my life I could handle something like that. I couldn't handle pimples on my face when I was a kid, I could never handle being second best in a tennis match, but I had no problems with people calling me an addict.

I stayed sober all through the season. I got over a thousand letters that year from all kinds of people. I was openly talking about recovery on interviews and on TV. I was truly beginning to get the message out.

When I went back to basketball, I did it with the attitude that sobriety was the most important thing to me. I had finally realized I was more than a basketball player; I was a person. And I had intuitively learned how to stop competing once the game ended. I didn't have the same compulsion to compete in life. I was happy with my contract and with my place on the team. I finally realized when good was good enough. And I knew I had to continue to keep working on me.

I think the greatest challenge in going back to play basketball was that everybody said I wasn't going to be able to stay sober in that environment. Well, I knew that I could. I knew that people in recovery could go back to bad environments. It wasn't the lifestyle itself that had given me problems. I was the problem. This time when I went to Milwaukee, I was up there by myself, just like I'd been alone at Golden State and Washington. All that free time was available to me again, but now I had a life outside of basketball. It wasn't a problem anymore.

A big part of the life and my recovery was attending my Twelve Step meetings. I lived only a block from one and went every morning. They were a perfect setting where I could deal with problems and emotions that would come up. I visited counselors and found a meeting to go to in each city we played. After a couple times around the league, I had friends all over the country. I wasn't stuck in my hotel room any longer. People would come over, and we would go to meetings together.

I now had a nationwide treatment network. I had fellowship and friendship, and I was learning how to become responsible, doing sober things, and not drinking. Meetings also gave me opportunities to share my experience, and nothing felt better to me than to help people get into treatment or to have people come to talk to me or hear me speak.

I don't want to give the impression that I was on a journey to sober up the world. I wasn't. But I *was* on a journey to show the gift of sobriety and what it can do. I was really coming to see that none of what I was going through was enough reason to drink anymore. When I got sober, I grew up. I began to discover a lot of the things I missed as a kid. Just because I got on the piss pot backwards didn't mean I had to stay that way.

The first couple years in recovery, I took great pains to keep my personal life in order. I was always very conscious of how I looked. I became neat and very responsible. I tried very hard to be on time, and if I said I was going to do something, I did it. I was a very, very grateful recovering addict. I was a doormat to the world of sobriety. I thought, "I'm just glad I ain't drinking, and the rest of the you can just walk all over me, cuss me, scorn me — I don't care. As long as I ain't drinking, nothing else matters."

I was carrying this attitude a bit too far, and things changed for the better when I went out to buy a new car my first year back with the Bucks. I planned to buy a BMW 750 from a friend of mine at the time, and I had him order one. The wait for the car was longer than he had said. I looked around a bit and found one just like I was looking for in stock, and for a much better price. After I bought it, I called my friend and told him what I had done — and I asked him to return my earnest money. He refused, saying that they were going to keep it because I'd made them go out of their way to get my car.

For maybe the first time I really stood up for myself. I went down to his showroom and said I wasn't going to leave until I got my money. They called my family, and told them I'd had a relapse. They said that I was loud, that a policeman walked in and I got very nervous and then left. I didn't make an incident, I just wanted my money back.

This was when the recovery saying "I'm as good as anybody who's not drinking, as long as I don't drink" first made sense. I felt good about taking care of myself. What that guy wanted to do was wrong. He didn't care about me being out five thousand dollars and not getting a car, he just wanted to keep my money. Just because I was an ex-addict didn't give him any right to cheat me. But that's the one shot people can take at you — accuse you of drinking again. In the end, they gave all my money back.

I went through so much pain to recover because it was the one gift I had to give myself. I had to become responsible for me, even though I so much wanted somebody to coach me through it. I still wanted teammates and the roar of a crowd. When I finally got my first year of sobriety, after failing so many times, I thought I was going to get a gold watch or something, but all I got was another medallion!

Toward the end of the season, I realized that things were finally coming together for me. I'd gone from being an unemployed addict to playing again in the NBA. When the games ended, I had recovery. I had other activities outside of basketball that made me feel whole. I was putting my education to good use in my fitness company. God was doing for me what I'd never been able to do for myself.

For the first time in a long, long time, I was enjoying living. I was enjoying every day of my life. I had a balance that I'd never had before. I felt good about who I was. I knew what I was doing every day. I knew where I was waking up, I knew where I'd been, I knew who I'd been with, and what I'd said. Then one day, the realization hit me that I hadn't needed to apologize to anyone in a year.

Joyce Bossett

The important thing to John was that he was sober and that he could go back to the NBA and show them that he really wasn't a bad guy. We had a little scare with him, though, when the Bucks went into the playoffs. The team was in Philadelphia when John called and said, "I need to have a drug screen." I said, "Oh, my God, John, what for?" John laughed and told me not to worry, that it had been a long time since we'd been testing on a monthly basis, so he wanted someone independent to come up and test him so that we could have it on record that he was going into the playoffs absolutely clean of chemicals. We sent a nurse and an administrator from our hospital there to get a sample. Before the start of the game, the official report was in. John was clean.

We won fifty games that year but lost to Boston in the semifinals of the Western Conference playoffs. I averaged eighteen points for the season, the most ever in my career. I came back as a free agent, and at the beginning of the 1987-88 season, I signed another one-year contract with Milwaukee for the most money I'd ever been paid.

During this new season, however, I didn't play nearly as much as I was playing before. It wasn't a complete surprise, though, because already the year before I'd had to accept that I wasn't the center of attention anymore. I knew that I was getting older, and soon I'd be getting less playing time than I'd been used to. I was still a solid citizen of the team, however, and I had my old leadership role back. I wasn't drafted number one because of talent — it was because of leadership skills.

During my second year in Milwaukee, I introduced my fitness program to an HCA hospital there. Not long after that, we opened a treatment unit, too. I was there a lot, leading the fitness program, exercising, and helping with some groups. Debbie and the kids had moved to Milwaukee now, too, and life was going well. It was a similar structure to what I had in Houston — it was like having two homes that I could move between with ease.

I was enjoying helping other people, including some other athletes and coaches who'd gotten into trouble. The names are not important. What's important is that I could be there for them. I spent hours at people's homes, even on days of games. But it was for me too; I needed to get out of myself. Giving back to others became — and still is — a very important part of my own recovery.

Halfway into the 1987-88 season, Milwaukee decided to trade me to the Sonics. I didn't really care about the trade; I was just happy that somebody wanted me to play. I was getting to be an old pro who was still trying to do the job and couldn't accept that time was running out. I could be a member of the team, but I wouldn't have the active role I once had. A couple days after the trade was announced, I was in the locker room saying good-bye to all the guys, when one of the coaches came in and told me to put my things back. For salary cap reasons, I couldn't be traded. I finished the season with the Bucks.

When the season finally ended, however, I actually was traded to Seattle for the 1988-89 season. I wasn't angry, but I had trouble accepting my changing role. One of the hardest things I had to accept in recovery was realizing that I wasn't going to be a star anymore. My first year back, I was the main attraction, just like Dennis Rodman was his first year at San Antonio. Everybody wanted to talk to me, mainly because they were curious to see if I was going to be able to stay sober. My team was doing well, in large part because of my contribution when I took the place of an injured player. But the next year, I became a role player. I was the sixth or seventh man. I was still a pretty effective basketball player, but I wasn't a star anymore.

One of the biggest things I'm still working on is an acceptance of aging. I have a great fear of getting older. I turned forty not long ago. I'm getting balder and balder, and the balder I get, the blacker I dye my hair. That's a lack of acceptance. Here's a guy who once had no desire to live past thirty-five who's now scared of getting older and wants as much out of life as he can get!

When I was considering returning to basketball, my main concern was whether I could maintain my sobriety. A close second was the work I had begun in Houston with Joyce and HCA. I very much wanted to continue it. I loved helping people get sober and recover, and with Joyce's help, I remained very active and involved with my programs and projects.

Then in mid-1988, life dealt me what I felt was a tough blow. Joyce decided to leave Houston to go to HCA's business development corporate offices in Tennessee. Her resignation took me completely by surprise, and I really felt as though she had betrayed me. Of course Joyce had told me she wouldn't be in Houston forever. And I knew that things change and that I needed to find my own strength, but I kept telling Joyce that we had a bond that simply couldn't be broken.

Ultimately, Joyce went to Tennessee, but our relationship never changed. Everything I have done, I've discussed with Joyce. We are like a family. She's been the coach's coach, my mentor, and my business advisor. I continue to bring different deals to her for advice. We have a tremendous amount of trust between us. I feel I owe Joyce so much for trusting and taking a chance on me when I really needed a break. She helped me get my life back together by giving me a safe environment where I could live and grow. We were — and are — a great team. We're both good at coming up with new ideas, but I can't always get them on the table. Joyce is great at helping me articulate them. I am comfortable enough with her that I can come to her with anything I'm thinking, no matter how crazy, and she'll listen and help me evaluate it.

Joyce Bossett

After I left, we negotiated to name the chemical dependency wing after John because he was up there all the time, doing groups gratis, having community meetings with the staff, coming into early morning groups, bringing people to the meetings. He was all over the place. The hospital really became John's — the staff and the physicians were all so supportive of him.

John knew the business well, and the unit basically became his. He hired staff and worked closely with the physicians to make sure that the treatment approach met the needs of the different populations and that the athletes could incorporate their workouts into the program. He was very instrumental in the design of the program.

John was always trying to help other players who were having trouble with drugs. When he first began to get more involved with the center, he would ask for a player to come in for a weekend, or if we could just detox a guy. I helped John see that you can get a guy back on the court quickly, but maybe that's not the way to really help him. You want to get that guy back on the court when he's strong enough, when he understands what's going on with him, after he's participated in a program, and when he has a decent chance to stay sober. That's why he developed such an extensive program that would support the players at every stage of their recovery.

> *During the summer of 1988, John rented a couple of apartments so that the guys who had been in treatment during the year could participate in aftercare. This experience made him realize that he needed a permanent house where he could have a social worker, therapists, and counselors to provide therapy for the guys. So he bought one. His residential treatment center is called The House, and it's become a key component of his work.*

More and more athletes were coming to Houston to get treatment in my center. Maybe no one better understands how much these guys need good aftercare than I do. I just didn't have the space to keep putting them in my own apartment, so I bought a townhouse in a very plush Houston neighborhood to use for a halfway house. Now remember, the people I was bringing in to live there were all millionaire athletes. Economically, they fit the neighborhood, but that didn't matter to my neighbors. They blew a gasket. They didn't want drug addicts or people like that in *their* neighborhood. That was the first time I'd ever felt any form of prejudice in my work with recovering athletes. But ten years ago, being a drug addict was like being infected with HIV today. It was just such a taboo.

When that happened, I stopped to ask myself why I was doing all this — causing trouble for myself, working so hard to help these people. Well, because I'm one of them and because we aren't bad people; helping people recover had become a passion. Today there are a still lot of people who don't accept somebody in recovery until it happens to them or someone they love. It's odd. But when it's their daughter or husband or brother, then they have a different perspective on what it means to be a recovering person. Regardless of what other people thought, I continued to bring players like Lloyd Daniels down to Houston for treatment in my center.

Lloyd Daniels, guard, San Antonio Spurs
When I got to Houston, what John told me was this: "Lloyd,

all you have to do is follow the program and do the work; I'll take care of the rest." Now what people don't realize is that you can have everybody in the world that wants to help you, but if you're not willing to take the extra step, you ain't never going to be clean. That's how I look at it. You got to be the one that wants to stop. At that point, I finally decided I got to do something. I wasn't going nowhere.

I just was impressed at how Lucas was doing it. He stayed around clean people and he worked the program. I learned from him that that's what you've got to do. You can't hang out with guys that use, thinking you're not going to use. You've got to leave them old places alone. You can be willing to stay clean and sober, but you need to replace your old ideas and old beliefs with something new. That's real hard because at first I didn't know what to replace the old with. You become confused. That's how the meetings help — they let you find people who are clean and sober, people who are willing to help you and give you some direction about what way to carry your life so that you can become this new person.

To be really honest, when I first started going to meetings, I hated them. I said to myself, "Why am I going with all these old people? They don't know what they're talking about." But what I learned is, meetings are part of the program because if you don't go to meetings and hang around them old-time people, people who've been there before you, you are going to relapse. And after a while, going gets to be a habit. It grows on you if you're going all the time. And then things start to change.

John Lucas helped me see that what I needed to do was change those beliefs of mine that were creating emotional and financial and physical problems for me. So that's what I did. You have to get to know and take care of this new person. That's difficult because we addicts don't know how to do that at first. We don't have any past experience of doing it. I found a release in the meetings and in associating with people who are recovering and who are walking like they're talking. That to me is the beginning of the recovery process.

I quit getting high. I learned that you don't have to get high to have fun, to go bowling, to shoot pool, go to movies. I always thought that if I do those type of things, I got to have a joint in my hand or a beer. I'm not scared anymore to have a birthday without getting high. That's how things have changed. When I go to a restaurant to eat or to meet with a media guy or something, I don't have to have a beer or a martini to talk to him. I'm not fearful anymore. I can meet and talk to new people and feel comfortable. That really makes me proud of myself.

Sometime when I sit in these hotel rooms when I'm on the road, I say, "Lloyd, you are lucky just to be alive." It's amazing and I'm grateful. I just sit back and remember in those old CBA days. I'd be creeping, taking drinks, going to clubs, hanging out. But I don't need that any more because I know I'm going to die if I do that.

A lot of addicts don't realize who they are, because when they're using, all they're doing is chasing, drinking beer, smoking dope, staying up all night, lying to people and really lying to themselves. But once you get clean and sober, you get to find out who you are. You might have a long way to go to get there, but at least you get to know day by day who you are. I'm starting to know Lloyd Daniels, understand Lloyd Daniels. I'm a guy who learned how to be by himself. I don't need to run with that crowd no more because that crowd ain't doing nothing.

Playing pro ball ain't an easy life, period. What people don't realize is that you've got to perform every night. You can't come out there high stepping. It's a real long season. Once you've been in the NBA for a while, you realize that hey, this is your job. It's your business, you got to take care of it or you could be gone.

And then there's all the temptations. Especially when you

come to a big city like Los Angeles, it's easy to get caught up thinking that you should go out and be chasing. And people can know you're clean but they'll still try to get you to use with them. They try to bring that bad stuff back out. You got to really be careful. That's when I got to know to pick up the phone and call my friends. You always can have somebody to talk to, someone who can help you. So John was right. He had the program, and I'm doing it.

Seeing guys like Lloyd getting a new life and getting back to their careers really make me feel great. As much as I love to help people recover from addiction, I get even more joy from working with kids to help prevent them from getting on this road in the first place.

Joyce Bossett

About the time John first began working with us, we came up with the idea for an organization we called STAND, Students Taking Action Not Drugs. Over the next few months, a fellow we hired was trying to organize the program for us. It became apparent, unfortunately, that he just didn't have the wherewithal to do the job. He wasn't recovering, and he couldn't really identify with people who were struggling with this problem.

One day in a staff meeting, someone said we needed to find the right person to get STAND up and running. I said, "Give me the phone." I called John and asked him to join us in the meeting. He walked in not knowing exactly what to expect, and I guess I surprised him pretty good when I asked, "How would you like to be president of the STAND organization?" Well he hadn't heard of it, but after we talked about it, he said, "Oh, yeah, that sounds great!"

We just gave him the whole thing — we said take it, set it up, get schools enrolled, get some adult advisors. He just took the ball and ran. STAND became John's baby, and today it is still very successful.

I built STAND into a crisis center first, but then we expanded the services it provided. We developed a hot line for teens that offered crisis and emergency counseling by phone, and we helped kids in some of the Houston schools start some peer support groups.

My work in prevention led me to become the initial impetus for the programs that were put in place when the NBA and the NBA Players Association finally began to deal with the whole drug issue. I've been involved ever since in helping the league and the Players Association develop them.

Charles Grantham, executive director,
National Basketball Players Association

I was the player rep when John first admitted his problem with drugs. Looking back, it's amazing to see how much denial the league and most of our nation were in. But in 1982, the L. A. Times dropped a bomb that blew everything wide open. They published an article claiming that 75 percent of NBA players had used cocaine. You can imagine the reaction to that! Fans were turned off and the league had a real PR problem on its hands. Regardless of the validity of the number, that article did two very positive things: not only did it grab America's attention, it grabbed ours, too. We had to get our butts out of denial and do something about this problem.

John has played a key role in the development of the league's drug policy, treatment, and education programs, and he was helping us even when he was the most public problem guy.

One of the first things John taught us was that if a person is addicted, he's going to figure out some way to get his drug. After he first admitted his use, John, his agent, and I decided to put bodyguards with him to keep him away from drugs. Looking back, I don't know what we were thinking: one way or the other, John's going to get it. And he did. John helped us see that we had to separate guys from their jobs for a while if change is going to occur.

The league and the players worked together for nearly two years to develop a policy on dealing with drugs. John and a few other guys were slipping through the cracks at this time and not getting the help and support they needed because we didn't know what was best to do yet.

At first the owners wanted to have regular random testing for everybody. Well, that wouldn't work because just as you can't go search somebody's house without just cause, you can't search someone's body either. We said, however, that if the league president and all the owners and their staffs agreed to participate as well, we'd agree. End of that idea!

It's very important to see this discussion in context. The whole country was trying to understand this problem and deal with it. We spent countless hours trying to get people to understand that this was an illness, that when an employee is sick, you don't just fire him and ban him permanently from his profession. You try to help him. We said that this was like any illness — sometimes an illness can be bad enough that employees have to stay home from work for a time while they get well. These were new concepts to a lot of people involved. It took time for the league and the owners to realize that there were a lot of costs involved: a financial cost to the owners if a player on his team is using drugs; the obvious human cost to the player and his family; and finally, a cost to the league and the community.

Through the work of many people, including John and other players involved with drugs and recovery, we eventually came up with the "one, two, three strike" plan — which included a comprehensive education and counseling component.

We first created a moratorium period during which those individuals who already had problems could come forward for help without penalty. We offered them support, a confidential treatment program, a testing program, and ongoing counseling to help them develop a drug-free lifestyle. When forty-eight players came forward to go through the drug program, we realized that we had a lot of cleaning up to do.

After that period, the policy went into effect. With the first strike, the player voluntarily comes forward, receives help (paid for by the league), and still gets his salary. For his second offense, the player is suspended without pay, but still gets help. The third time, the player is banned for life — but with an opportunity to reapply to play after two years. Neither the league nor the players really wanted to end a guy's career for good. We always wanted to leave the door open for a guy to come back if he could get his life together.

John's more formal help in all of this came later once he became sober, but I remember telling him and a couple other guys who were addicts, "One of you guys will be the salvation of our policy. Someone's going to have to come through our program, deal with the illness, and then finally grab on to sobriety and succeed enough so that others will want to imitate him." And John was that guy. All the other help he's given us aside, the example of his sobriety alone has led many people into recovery.

I think that the "one , two, three strike" policy is fair, but I stressed early on with Charlie just how important it was to have an educational component in the program, too. We really worked hard on this while I was in recovery and still playing. I helped him understand the challenges of overcoming the odds, what it took for me to get sober. He had to know what that fight was all about before an effective policy could be developed. We needed to have as many recovering athletes as possible speaking out, talking to the players. We've always shared the belief that we have to help guys understand addiction. They need to understand that once a player is addicted, he's not just trying to have a good time anymore. That's not the issue. It's a sickness. We needed to talk about the pro lifestyle, how you can be seduced into using, how you can finally be addicted, and how once that addiction is there, it is out of your control.

Two years of work with my programs in Houston, along with playing again, helped me develop an aftercare program that I thought would help the NBA. I wanted us to go beyond treatment and education. Charlie and I began working closely to talk about the advantages of a more complete and formal aftercare program. Joyce and I put together a training manual and presented it to Charlie. At the time, the NBA players went to Van Nuys for treatment, but once the program was accepted, the players could go either there or to Houston for treatment, and to my center in Houston for aftercare. These different components came together out of my past need for them. I knew that if aftercare like this could help me, it was bound to benefit others. It was a way to help guys stay in recovery. All of this was exciting for me, not only because of what we were creating, but because I was really using my education.

Another program I had a big part in getting installed — and this was also based directly on my own experience when I came back to play — was the nationwide support network for recovering players. As I told Charlie and the league, when I tried to get sober the first times, I didn't have the help I needed. All of a sudden I was traveling around again and there's guys around trying to sell me drugs and I'm back to all my old connections. A guy trying to make a change needs help if he's going back to *that* environment.

The league eventually set up a system modeled on the one Joyce and HCA had set up for me. There are counselors in each city for these guys while they're on the road. The support network, along with education, of course, was very important because they gave the players help and they demonstrated that we really cared about them as people. And, of course, it gave them something to hold on to at a time when things would get shaky.

Bobby Carter, NBA drug counselor

This program is about us addicts helping each other. When I call on a guy or I come to see him, I don't come to see him as the great basketball player, I come to see him as a brother, a human being. We can talk about whatever we need to, and it doesn't have to be about basketball. We talk about the program, about keeping our lives together and doing the things that we need to do on a daily basis without drinking and using, about trying to be the best person that we can be.

The only guarantee in life is that there are no guarantees. That's what we have to deal with. This can be real frightening, especially for a guy who has a family and things are a little out on the edge. Life can be real stressful, especially for someone who is recovering and maybe looking for excuses to drink and use.

At the beginning and close of the season, we get all the guys together and check to see how they're doing. If there are any problem areas that they need to talk about, I see if we can help find solutions.

Then during the season, when the fellows come into town (I live in the Los Angeles area), I make an effort to call them and see how they're doing. I'll try to come see them, maybe go out to lunch, take them to a meeting if it's possible.

The players love to have this kind of contact. We're trying to show that we care for them as individuals, and I find that most players need this kind of attention — they need to know that someone is there for them or that there's someone they can call when there's a problem. These guys are on the road a lot, but they don't necessarily have a good friend in each city. Knowing who to trust becomes a problem. The basketball court is their world and they can protect themselves there, but once they get off of that court, they have to be very careful. That's why we're here for them.

Given the lifestyles and the career span of our players, I felt that the earlier we could get to our players with information — and help, if necessary — the better. That meant we needed to have a program specifically designed for rookies. We wanted all of them to understand from the beginning of their careers the importance of a drug-free lifestyle.

Now, I thought we needed to test our rookies, but this created a problem at first because we don't have mandatory random testing in the league, except for those players who are recovering. Players could only be tested if there was suspicion of use. But my point was this: if some guys are coming in with drug problems, let's find out right away. Then maybe we can help them before they end up like I did. The players association thought this made sense and granted the league the right to randomly test rookies. If a rookie tests positive, we don't ban him, we don't even call it a first strike. Instead, they're out for the whole season and we have them in the program, which gives us time to really work with them.

Rod Thorn, NBA vice president of operations

We started the rookie transitional program/aftercare program in the mid-1980s because we found that most of the players who ended up with a substance abuse problem had the problem when they came into the league. It wasn't something they acquired after they got here. More than that, however, we were seeing kids who were having other problems, too — with agents, with their families, with money, with all kinds of things. As you can imagine, coming to the pros is a huge transition for any twenty-year-old. Things can happen when you suddenly become very rich!

We had a crying need for the program, to tell the truth, and John's help with it has been invaluable. All the rookies coming into the league meet for three days at some site — it's been Dallas or Orlando recently. It's designed first to get them thinking about situations they'll soon face, and second, to give them some ideas about how to handle themselves.

We get them to look at how to deal with a new situation, for example, with family, with someone on your team who may be doing drugs, with having money for the first time.

They work with psychologists, ex-players, Drug Enforcement Administration members, and doctors from places like Johns Hopkins. We talk about everything from involvement in drugs to AIDS.

I am always very impressed with the message John has. Players can identify with somebody who had gotten off the track and then had gotten himself back together. John talks about what happened to him and how he thought he could beat it. How he "just knew" that any time he got ready to quit, he could. How you can't beat this stuff. That it doesn't help you. That it could happen to anybody. John delivers a very powerful message.

I am pleased to say, too, that the program has been very successful. No rookie has tested positive — either coming in or during his season — in the last three years.

My work with the treatment centers and with the NBA complemented each other perfectly. Things just kept falling into place. My idea for The House, as you can see, was just a natural next step when dealing with recovering people, especially professional athletes.

About this time, too, I began to realize there might be one more way we could help ease these players back into their profession. I wondered, What if you could have a team where players could recover and still be playing ball. Could you somehow imitate the pro lifestyle for the players while still providing the support and aftercare they need? This seemed like an ideal next step, but I couldn't see how to get it done yet.

Seattle had a pretty good season the year I played for the Sonics. We even beat the Rockets in the playoffs. I only played a little, however, and they didn't re-sign me. I still hoped I could play one more year, and in the off-season, I signed for the 1989-90 season, my fourteenth in pro ball, with guess who? The Houston Rockets. Now this was the team that told me four years earlier that I would never, ever play for their organization again. And now they re-signed me.

When I came back to Houston that year, it was a real homecoming for me. I had a sense of having come full circle. What's more, I had all kinds of things going on for me. I had a unit that had been dedicated to me, the John Lucas Treatment and Recovery Center. I had three other treatment programs running in the city. My company, John H. Lucas Enterprises, was growing and already employed fifteen or twenty people. We specialized in drug and alcohol education, treatment, rehabilitation.

I had thrown my heart into this Twelve Step work, trying to find affordable care for people, to get them the help they need. I wanted to be there for others. I was always an assist guy in basketball, in the top-five all time for assists, but now I was giving people assists in life, and there's nothing like that. I didn't get sober to stay in meetings and drink coffee. I got sober to get on with my life. I wanted a plan for living and to move forward, that's what I got.

That year with the Rockets, I played a lot again and eventually started regularly. One day I ran into Bill Fitch. We had a little conversation, and I told him how much he had taught me about living. To this day I will say that Fitch saved my life because he was willing to kick me off the team. That made me stop using because I finally realized I didn't have any more chances. Bill told me that when he saw how I was helping other kids who were in trouble, he knew this was my role. "It's what you're here for, John," he said. And he was right about that, too.

Near the end of the season, I pulled a hamstring and was put on injured reserve. I knew it was time to quit, and I did. My career as a basketball player was finally over. I felt sad, certainly, but I had so much else now in my life that it didn't really bother me that much — and that in itself showed me just how far I had come.

CHAPTER 8

THE TROPICS

More and more athletes, especially basketball players, were coming to Houston for treatment in my program, and from my own experience, I knew that good aftercare was a key to maintaining their recovery. But they needed more than that. When people from other professions — doctors, electricians, teachers, mechanics — come through treatment, they can normally return to their professions, though sometimes under supervision. But for the NBA players who came to us, it was a different story. With the "one, two, three strike" rule, a lot of these guys were banned for two years or life, so they had to wait a long time to go back to their profession.

Even though most pro ball players went to college, many didn't finish. Without college degrees or commonplace work experience, they were unable to find any decent jobs. They weren't qualified and had no experience. So I knew we had to come up with a way to get them back working — and that meant playing basketball. I felt we needed to create an *basketball* environment in which the players could demonstrate not only their skills, but also their sobriety.

Too often the media say — and they certainly said this about me often enough — that the problem for a guy was the people he was with, the places he went, and what he did — the basketball environment, in other words. They say that basketball isn't the best environment for these people. Well, sure, the basketball life gives a guy plenty of opportunity to get and use drugs. Some do, but not everybody uses. I did both: played and used, played and didn't use. The environment isn't the problem, *they're* the problem.

I have always believed that once we got someone into recovery, they at least had a chance to work again in basketball — even though some of them didn't believe that themselves. They thought their lives were over, that they would never, ever play again. I knew that the "trust in your Higher Power" concept might be too much to put on them at first, so instead I told them, "Don't ever shortchange recovery. You just stay sober and anything can happen." I was trying to teach them that once you got yourself straight, you're as good as the next person and anything can happen. Get on with your life and see what comes.

As part of our aftercare, then, I began to help guys find jobs. I called some USBL teams for one guy who'd been a coach, and I said, "I'll give you a free coach if you'll just give him an opportunity to work. He'll be a great coach, better than people you have working for you now. Just give him a chance." So Kevin Mackey, the coach at Cleveland State, stayed sober, and I got him a job with the Atlanta Eagles. I even offered to pay the salary if the club would just give these guys a chance.

Thinking about my players, I said to myself, "Here I am in Houston with some of the best players in world, guys who are looking for an opportunity to get back to pro ball. How can I help them do that?" Then it hit me. The summer leagues. In different parts of the country, you have summer basketball leagues that usually run about an eight-week season. You often see guys playing to work on their game, to keep in shape, and to have a little fun. So I started getting my guys into this summer organization.

These leagues are not only a good way to play and stay in shape, they're a great chance for people to showcase themselves before the NBA draft or to NBA scouts. So I would call and get six or seven NBA scouts to come through every other week or so to watch who we had down here play against the teams in Houston because so many pros lived in Houston. What I was really trying to do was make recovery become a little fun. And despite the NBA's aftercare program, downtime for us is in the summers. It's a time when guys have a lot of time and the chance for relapse is big.

In late 1991, my friend Mackey, then a coach with a USBA team named the Miami Tropics, called me with a great suggestion. He said, "John, you're always looking for ways to get your guys playing ball again. Well, the Tropics are for sale. Why don't you buy the team? It would be a great component for your aftercare program." I looked into it and quickly realized that it could be just what I was looking for. We wanted to see what we could do, so I went ahead and coached the Tropics that year, and the next year I bought them.

When I took over the Tropics, the first thing I did was look at how the team would be set up. I had ten positions to work with, so I decided that six would go to former professional players who were out for the year because they had tested positive for drugs while playing in the CBA or the NBA. The four other slots would go to rookies, and when we drafted, I took only players who were recovering or had been at risk at some time.

Next I looked beyond the players to the organization itself. I tried to run it as much like an NBA office as I could, because I also wanted to use the team as an avenue for other recovering people who had gotten in trouble — front office staff, for instance — to pull themselves back up. There are other people in the sport besides players who are trying to recover and need a job, too, so we tried to keep this in mind when we hired. Everybody in the club, from the president and owner on down, were people in recovery.

The Tropics fit very well into my athletes aftercare program. It blended intense daily workouts with psychological and career counseling. My work was to help players find a sense of self-worth outside of sports. The game doesn't last forever, but for most of these guys, it's their only identity.

That first year's team could have beaten some NBA teams. We were *good*. We had Roy Tarpley of the Dallas Mavericks, Grant Gondrezick of the L. A. Clippers, Richard Dumas of the Rockets, Pearl Washington of the New Jersey Nets, and guy named David Robinson [not the David Robinson of the Spurs], just to name some. All our games were on Sunshine Cable, which was great for player exposure. We would be seen around the country, and even prime time and local TV picked our team up and put our games on the air.

I lived and traveled with the team as I tried to create a small-scale version of the day-to-day environment — including the temptations — that big-league athletes face. For the eight-week season, I led daily therapy sessions, administered drug tests, and chauffeured the guys on road trips, driving a van as far as 750 miles at a clip.

Everybody on my team got paid the same amount of money, from the trainer to the number one guy: $300 a week. The idea was this — with only $300 for them to pay their bills and to live on each week, I was trying to teach money management skills, and humility. If you don't think *that* will instill a bit of humility and make them feel what they've lost, remember that we had guys who had been making $3 million a year before they lost their jobs. Not only are they not playing in the NBA anymore, they're playing in a summer league in front of three or four hundred people at most and making eighteen-hour rides in a little van to play games. That's like a doctor or lawyer going to work at a fast-food joint!

Poor Roy Tarpley. That man used to go crazy sometimes. He'd say to me, "Hey, dog, I can't be taking a beating like this for $277 dollars at the end of each week. You're nuts!" One time we spent thirty hours going to Atlanta and back, and Roy had to sit the whole way with one leg straight out because he was coming off ACL surgery. When we got back Roy said, "I'm never going to do this again." And then someone else just yelled at him, "Hey, Roy, you want breakfast? Where do you want to stop? Yeah, how about McDonald's?" Roy just broke up.

Dirk Minniefield, strength coach, San Antonio Spurs
John and I played against each other in the NBA. I was playing with Cleveland when John was with the Bucks, and ironically, I was the guy selected to replace John when he got suspended for the last time at Houston.

I came to the Tropics because I had gotten into trouble

with my own drug habit and landed in jail. When I got out, my former college assistant coach got in touch with John to help me out. I called John and told him what I wanted, and he told me that I could get it all back if I was really willing to stop. I was, so I went to Houston to go through his center. When I finished with treatment, I played ball with John's guys in the summer leagues, and then became an assistant coach for John with the Tropics the year he bought the club.

Now it's one thing to go through treatment, but when you're with the Tropics, you're really back in the same environment that you had trouble with in the first place. The whole thing started out as a trick to get guys to want to get sober. John took treatment and put it in basketball. That's all it really was — we were in treatment. John ran a tight ship for what a guy had to do to get his life and his basketball career back. Still, it was a lot of fun. It was like having your big brother coaching, because John was like a brother to us. He was great to have there, because like he always said, he knows how it feels when people give up on you.

On a typical day, we'd get up at 5:30 A.M. and begin the day with a workout; 7:00 A.M., a Twelve Step meeting; 8:30 A.M., group therapy; 10:00 A.M., we'd tape and go to practice. Practices were long and hard with a lot of running because a lot of the players were out of shape. After practice was over, some guys would get urine tests. We did random drug testing. Then we would go back and have another group session, though maybe not quite as long as the first one. The guys could pretty much do what they wanted after that, though they still had to attend one more Twelve Step meeting, either later in the afternoon or early evening. Game days were easier, and I'd let them rest some. Curfew was midnight.

The atmosphere was really no different than any other basketball team. The only difference is that we were all more involved with each other's lives. In professional basketball, guys really don't get to be close.

This team didn't have any choice about that. We had to be close to survive because everybody was watching us. I have to say, that first year's team was one of the closest I've ever been on.

I'm not going to tell you that everything went perfect, that nobody slipped. People did. I can't tell when a guy is ready for recovery. Only he knows. We dealt with slips like we deal with everything else. I had to send a guy home because he just wasn't doing it right. He didn't want to follow the guidelines. But I still help him today. That part just didn't work out. Maybe it will someday.

Dirk Minniefield

Some people really took the program to heart and it really worked for them. Not everybody's going to do it the first time, of course. We had some younger guys who hadn't lost enough. So everything wasn't always smooth. What we had was ten addicted people who, as professional athletes, had done everything their way and all of a sudden someone's telling them they can't do all those things their way any more. It was a battle every day. At first, guys were just going out and partying, getting drunk.

There was a lot of relapse the first month we were there. Hell, we were in Miami, one of the easiest places in America to get cocaine. It wasn't like they were all choirboys. It wasn't intended to be like that. The intent was to help you get through those situations that got you into the most trouble, to learn how to live without using cocaine or any other substances. John is trying to teach people how to live without destroying themselves.

One time, a couple of guys had been out all night drugging, and we were supposed to fly out at 6:00 A.M. John came in, took one look at them, and said, "Damn, what am I going to do with you?" He had the rest of us go ahead, and left a couple guys behind to kind of help get those two back to a normal state. Later that day, they caught a flight and arrived in time for the game. One guy involved wound up getting fifty points that night. He said, "You see, I don't have to stop this shit." So the next night, John benches him — just to let him know that it wasn't about basketball, it's about your life.

Any professional athlete who makes a lot of money can get away with a lot of shit if he wants to. But there's nothing that those players can't do or say that John hasn't said or done already. He always cuts them off at the pass. I tried that myself for a while, but I found out I was going up the wrong tree. This guy's already been there.

A couple months later during a summer league game, one of the guys scored forty-five or fifty points, but then that night he went out and relapsed. John turned the decision about what to do over to the team. The player who relapsed was our leading scorer, and we needed him to win. What did we decide? The team feeling was, yes, this guy's a big part of the team and we want him to play, but we also want to help his life. So we wouldn't let him play.

This is what the Tropics are all about — helping guys with their lives. At first, it was really tough to differentiate between basketball and living, but that's what the team was based on, and that's the way we approach it. And it's what means the most to John.

I know I'm not powerful enough to keep anybody from drinking or taking drugs. But I will always be there to help. We just continue to build. It's not how many chances you get, it's how many times you keep trying. It's the guy who gives up on himself that scares me, because that means he's lost the will to live. This is a progressive disease, so if you don't quit, you're going to die. I'm always willing to help the person who honestly keeps trying to get himself sober. I don't care how many times it takes. When is enough, enough? Never!

I have seen a lot of people go through multiple treatments, and in owning and coaching the Tropics, I think I discovered why that happens. In a treatment setting, they see so much love and support that when they leave and they don't have it, they screw up to get back. When they're out, they get lonely, they miss everyone, and they are now with people who are different. I tell these guys all the time, "You're only different if you think you're different. You're different when you drink or do drugs. You can leave the drinking behind and still have all those good feelings."

We won maybe thirteen games in a row that first year, and we took the league championship. But we faced a lot of challenges, too, and I don't just mean slips and relapses. The team didn't get the exposure it deserved, although I understood why. The team's previous owners hadn't paid their bills and generally had a bad reputation, so I took over a club that had not been handled in the best way as far as the city was concerned. I also don't think the city believed me when I told them about all the things I was going to do. They wanted to know who else was helping me get this thing set up. And they had trouble believing that I didn't have any hidden motives.

I really caught a lot of flack at the press conference in Miami when I announced my intent to buy the team. One sportswriter asked how I felt about having people who'd fallen astray back out there in the limelight, implying, of course, that these players didn't deserve to be back. My answer to this guy was simply this: "If one of these guys was your kid, what would you want somebody to do? Yeah, you'd want somebody to help him. Just because there's been a mistake made doesn't mean these guys have to be buried for life." I told them that I really believe we aren't bad people, we just made some wrong choices.

I've lost a lot of money in being involved with the Tropics, too, not that making money was my goal. You need sponsors to run a team, and because we're talking about recovery here, I wouldn't take sponsors who sold alcohol. They're very hard find; so much advertising in sports is alcohol-related.

My goal wasn't to make money or to win championships. It was to get guys sober and back to work. It's never just the game. It's about character. I tell them all the time, "Basketball is a window on your soul." In this sense, we have been very successful. The first year, ten guys got sober and got jobs, either in Europe or in the NBA. I built up a strong network of people in the United States, Europe, and other areas to help find people jobs.

Getting coaches or scouts to look at my guys took time, too, because too many people in the league didn't trust me right away. I would tell somebody, "This guy could play for you. He deserves a chance to try out for the team, so would you bring him to camp?" Initially the answer would be, "I don't have a spot for him." I think my honesty scared a lot of people away. They couldn't believe that there wasn't some gimmick there. They are all in the "Sports is competition, I got to beat you" mentality, so they couldn't believe that somebody would just give them a player. I was only trying to give some guys an opportunity, but everybody was thinking, "Hey, wait a minute! Why would Lucas be willing to help me?" Well, I wasn't trying to help their team, I was trying to help my guy get his life back, that's all. It's too bad, but a lot of people just couldn't see that.

The second year, 1993, we had two players back. Other guys wanted to come back, but I told them that running the Tropics is not about having the players come back every year. The idea is to get here and get out by getting a job in basketball again. I did feel, however, that I needed to bring back a couple of guys to help the new guys and to set the tone.

Both years with the Tropics were better than I ever anticipated. I really knew what we could do on the basketball side, and I knew the group therapy part could help, but I never thought some guys could come so far. Everybody was participating. Guys were getting honest, and one great thing was that I saw relationships coming back. A guy's girlfriend would come to stay in Miami. Mothers and fathers would come down to be with their sons. We got families in family groups. Not only did guys stop using and drinking, but family and other relationships that had been cut off for a long time would come back. We even had a wedding — one of our rookies got married. We held the service at halftime during a game right down on the court! It was televised in a couple million homes. Our players sang and I gave the bride away. That was a really great moment for us.

That second year, we again won the league championship, but it wasn't as easy as it was the first time, because these guys were a little older. But being older also made them more solid in their recovery than the first year's team, so it wasn't so hard in that sense. Most younger guys — not all, but a lot of them — still need to lose more before they are ready to change.

We made some changes, too. We are always learning how to do this better. One of the things I did was stop making the athletic component of our treatment program too cozy, because then the players had no reason to leave. I wanted them to be irritable enough to want get out. I also learned that you always have to keep monitoring your program, especially something like the Tropics, because the athletes get smarter and smarter.

Dirk Minniefield

The greatest thing that came out of my experience with the Tropics was that I learned there is no basketball without sobriety. You see, my problem wasn't that I couldn't play, it was that I got high. We athletes, especially basketball players, misconstrue things. We think that we only get judged on our play. We try to ignore the getting high part. So what happens is that you resist or resent what people in authority in basketball are telling you. You think if you can perform on the court, that's all that matters — especially for the young guys. They're always saying, "Hey, I should be able to do what I want." Well, it don't work that way — and when you get busted a couple of times, this realization begins to set in. And that's what John helped me to see.

I had been playing against John, a guy I idolized for a lot of years. Now suddenly I have a chance to learn a lot from him about life. And I got a friend, somebody I probably would never have talked to before, because I competed against him. That's the other thing that we addicts have to learn. Just because we compete doesn't mean we can't be friends.

There are not a whole lot of professional athletes who are not only teammates but friends. They work together on the floor, but when the games are over, they all go their separate ways. Athletes find a way to compete in everything. Especially guys who play the same position, because they are in competition with each other for their jobs.

John always stressed to us to let the competition stay on the floor. We don't have to compete in other ways. As much as I competed against John in the past, I wouldn't want to compete with him now, because I know it's detrimental to me — and the same goes for him. That doesn't mean we won't try to be the best we can be, but it does mean that we don't have to try to kill each other.

I'd like to be a coach some day, and John has been encouraging me on that, too. My second year with the Tropics, John hired me as an assistant coach, and it was a great chance to be with him in another way. I learned how it feels to try to understand your players. He always tells me, "Dirk, man, you got to always remember how coaches made you feel — you don't want to coach these guys like that." He says coaching is about listening to the players. Most coaches don't ever let you say nothing. Now I've been there, and I know you can't be a good basketball player without having some smarts. Smart coaches listen to their players.

Next, John says, you got to make the team feel like it's more than just a coach and players relationship. It's that you genuinely care about them. And that's the gift that John has: he can make people believe that he genuinely cares. And he does care. Caring doesn't mean making excuses for guys or never cutting them. No, it means being fair and being honest. Like John says, fair and honest aren't always pleasant, but when you're dealing with twelve recovering dope fiends, they understand.

Playing and working at the Tropics goes beyond player and coach because we are looking at guys who have been through the hell. With John, life transcends the job. The job doesn't transcend life.

Owning and coaching the Tropics is fun for me. I don't do it to promote John Lucas. I just saw where there was a need, and I tried to do something about it. I did this for me. It's not the same level as the NBA, but I like it because it keeps me close to my roots — helping people.

I'm not trying to set an example for others who are trying to recover. I'm just trying to stay sober. I have no ultimate purpose in my recovery other than to live my life drug-free. I realize that I've become a very visible recovering person. But that's God's work; I didn't ask for it and it's not my deal. I used to play tennis and basketball, now I help people. Coaching the Tropics has broadened my perspective on the ways I could inspire others in recovery. It taught me that basketball is an extension of what I do. I enjoy working with other people; it's like a vacation for me. I'm always learning. Some people learn by reading or taking classes. I learn by helping people.

So I do the Tropics for my recovery first, but it also helps me become a better coach. It helps me to remember that I can always improve. And sure, I get a chance to look at talent that may not be seen by other teams, too.

What I was hoping to do was give the guys a system to work within. I always tell them, "You know what slips are. They mean that sobriety has lost its priority. It can never do that. You've got to remember that sobriety is our number-one priority. It comes before your wife, it comes before your family, it comes before basketball, it comes before Mom and Dad — because if you don't take care of that number-one priority, you'll never have any of those others."

CHAPTER 9

COACH OF THE SPURS

After the Tropics' 1992 season and the summer leagues had finished, I returned to Houston and a pretty busy schedule. I was involved with a bunch of projects: working with Joyce and JHL Enterprises on my drug treatment center work; providing drug education and prevention programs to the CBA and to each NBA team; traveling throughout the country to check on players who were in aftercare in my athletes assistance program; making contacts to help players from the Tropics and the summer leagues get placed on pro teams; troubleshooting for players who were trying to come back into the NBA; and running STAND.

Bob Bass and I had stayed touch over the years since the Spurs tried to sign me back when I was in college. Early in the fall of 1992, Bob was in Houston on business, so we decided to have lunch together. Just in passing, I said to him, "The next time you are in the market for a coach, please give me a chance to interview." I left it at that because I was really busy with a lot of things — and besides, the Spurs had just hired a new coach, Jerry Tarkanian, who'd been head coach at UNLV for many years.

Just before Christmas — December 17, to be exact — I got a phone call from Bob, and he asked me, "John, are you interested in coaching the Spurs?" I said, "What!!??" I thought it was some kind of joke. But he said no, he was serious. "Yeah," I said, "I'd be interested." He told me nothing had been decided, and that he'd call me back the next day after the Spurs' game. B. B. did call me back, and said, "John, we want you to be the coach of the Spurs."

Bob Bass

I was still working for San Antonio, and I'd see John nearly every summer. I would go over to Houston and spend a day with him, or he'd call me over to interview some player he had in rehab and maybe watch the guy play, or he'd have some player from the Tropics he'd want me to see. It was always good to see him, and everyone around the Spurs had continued to like him in spite of the problems he'd had.

Around Thanksgiving of 1992, Red McCombs, who was one of the owners of the Spurs then, told me to be on the look-out for a new coach because things weren't going too well for us. He said we had to be thinking about what we need in case we had to make a change. So one day I just had this idea to call John. I thought, "So what if he's thirty-nine years old — really young to be a head coach in the NBA — and has very little coaching experience. I've got to see what he'd say."

I called John, and said, "John, what do you think about coaching?" Of course he was very excited about it. I went back to Red McCombs and said, "I know you're going to think I'm crazy, but I tell you, with the way he communicates and the way he works with people, John Lucas might be a great coach for our team. There are a lot of things he's done in basketball. I've seen him with the guys he helps and the players on his summer teams, and he's just really a people person. All the players relate to him, not only as a player but as a coach, too. He's very competitive, and he can instill that spirit into people who are around him. John's seen it all and he's done it all in that rehab business, and that's why he is well prepared to coach this team."

Well, Red looked at me and thought a bit, and then he said, "You know what? I believe you've got something." Those were his exact words: "I believe you've got something."

We didn't do anything for two weeks or so after that, but I stayed in contact with John, calling him every three, four days. Then all of sudden, Red tells me, "I need to change. You need to get ahold of Luke and see if he wants to coach our team and if he can."

When B. B. called me and offered me the coaching job, I didn't know what to say. I got on the phone with Joyce because I wanted the job, but I also wanted to keep the relationship I had with her and HCA. For the first time in my life, I had a life outside sports, a life and some strong work relationships that I liked very much and that had been important for my recovery. I wanted to make sure they could stay intact. And above all, I didn't want to coach if it would jeopardize my sobriety.

Joyce Bossett

I won't ever forget that day. It was in December, and I had taken off the afternoon to finish up my Christmas shopping when the phone rang in my car. It was John. I said, "What's wrong, John?" and he said, "B. B. is on his way to my office."

"Well," I said, "B. B.'s been to your office before, John, so what's up?" Then I asked him outright, "You're not going to go to San Antonio to coach, are you?"

"They made me an offer."

"Do you want to do it?" I asked him.

"That's why I'm calling you."

And I said, "Do you want to do this?"

"I think I'd do it for free."

"You probably would, but don't do it for free," I told him.

Then John wanted to know where I was going to be. I told him that I was on my way to finish my Christmas shop-

ping, and he asked me to take the phone along. He said, "I need to be able to talk to you until I leave." John called me four more times within half an hour. He wanted to know if he left, who'd take care of everything? I told him not to worry, that we could work everything out.

What did worry me was what would happen to the Tropics. He said, "Don't worry about that. I'll take care of them after the season's over with. But you have to promise me that you're going to take care of the business for me. Then I can go."

I said, "Okay, John, fine. I'll take care of it." Then I asked him if he knew where his wife was, and if he'd talked to her yet. He said he was trying to locate her. I said, "Call her, John, right now. Find her wherever she is and tell her." So he did, and then he was off to San Antonio.

Blond Lucas

When John called us about being the coach of the Spurs, I was totally shocked. He said, "Momma, where's Daddy? Get your hands on him right quick. We've got to talk because I need your opinion."

I said, "Well, John, you haven't been asking much lately for our opinion. What are you into now?" But he said, "Just get your hands on Daddy."

So I rode around looking for Lucas and finally found him at church. When we got back home, we got right on the phone to Houston. John said, "I've got an hour to make a decision, and I need you all to help me." Well, my heart was going thump-thump, and Lucas's was doing the same.

Then John said, "I've been offered the job of coach of the San Antonio Spurs."

There was a silence. Everybody just got quiet, and then John said, "You all still there? I've only got an hour, so let me know what to do."

We said, "Like we've always told you, John, the choice is yours. Whatever you do, we are going to be right there with you." So he said, "Okay, I have to tell them today. I have to get back to them today." Then Cheryl called, and we all got into a conference call with her. We discussed it, and she said, "I think it's great, John. Go for it!"

Lucas and I went out to eat and when we came back there was a message on the answering service. It was from John, and he said, "I did it." That's all he said. "I did it. Watch the game tonight."

Well, we watched the game and nothing was said about John. I've got to tell you, I nearly died during that game. The whole game and nothing had been said, and then when someone asked for the interview with Sean Elliott after the game, he said, "Our coach is in the locker room and it's John Lucas."

I nearly fainted. I lost all my feelings. I just went numb. I was wondering to myself whether he could really do it, but John had assured us he could. He said, "I'll handle it, I'll get it done." That was what he told us about his drug problem, too, and he did handle it.

When I saw him on TV that night, I was very happy for another reason. It seemed like John had finally recaptured all his old jubilance. The night he won his first game as a coach, we were watching on TV. When I saw John laugh, I saw a dimple I hadn't seen in years. I said, "Lucas, John is back almost all the way." I had been looking for that dimple for a long, long time. When he laughs real big, he makes that dimple, and I hadn't see it in years. But I saw it again that night.

Bob Bass

Red had to put the final okay on the deal, and he did. We brought John up to San Antonio that evening. We had a game that night with Dallas, and I wanted John to coach that game, without a practice, but Red said, "No, let's wait and let one of the assistant coaches coach the Dallas game." Then right after the game, we brought John in, and Red introduced him to the team as the new head coach.

I tell you, it was a great sight to see. Those players just fell off their chairs. They couldn't figure what in the world was going on there. They couldn't say anything. We shocked the NBA, too, when we did it! We took a thirty-nine-year-old guy who'd never even been an assistant coach and gave him one of the best teams in the NBA. Nobody could believe it.

Yeah, I just did it. I never discussed money or anything with Red, I just took the job. By hiring me, Red and B. B. knew they would be opening themselves up to criticism. Here they get a guy with *no* NBA coaching experience. I'd been out of pro ball since the 1990-91 season, when I retired as a player. Beyond that, I was known as one of the NBA's most notorious alcohol and cocaine abusers.

I came to San Antonio the night of the game, one that was being televised nationally. The club had announced that they had hired a coach, but nobody knew I was the man. I just sat in the arena and watched the game on the Jumbotron. Then after the game was done, I went down into the locker room. There were four guys there I had played with before and knew very well — Lloyd Daniels, Dale Ellis, Avery Johnson, Sean Elliott.

The guys knew there was a new coach, but when Red just walked in and gave me the job, they were *shocked.* The whole team was in a state of shock. I don't think they thought something would happen so quick, and then here they were bringing in someone new, someone no one had expected. This was so far out in left field that no one could possibly have anticipated that I would be the man.

But I was. Ever since I was a young kid, I've watched coaches and I've watched people. During my whole career as a player, I'd always had a desire to lead. Nothing gave me more satisfaction, even as a young kid, than to see someone else learn and accomplish something himself.

So I had this kind of experience and desire, and I had one more thing going for me. I had recovery and the principles of recovery — and I was not at this time about to sacrifice the principles of recovery just because I was coaching.

David Robinson

When John first came, we were obviously struggling. It was a big surprise to everyone when he was selected, and I didn't know John very well. To be honest, I was a little bit doubtful that he could do it. This was a situation where some really good coaches, like Larry Brown and Jerry Tarkanian, weren't able to extract all of our talent.

But a couple of guys on our team knew him, and they said he was a good guy and were excited about it. Avery Johnson thought it was a great move. And I was open to anything because we weren't winning.

John came in and was immediately more positive than any coach I've ever seen. He was just more upbeat. He supported the guys.

The first thing he said was, "You guys have all the talent you need to win right here in this room. You don't need any more talent. Everybody's talking about you don't have this, you don't have that. Well, we can win with what we have."

What he did was really begin to invest in us as people, and that's something that had really been missing ever since I'd come to the Spurs. The key was really getting guys to feel like the management believed in them. It's terrible to play feeling like you're always on the trading block or that your job is never secure. You can't expect anybody to play consistently under those conditions. There's got to be somebody on the team that the club feels confident about, and they've got to make those guys feel that way. The Spurs never did a good job of that. You can't just treat everybody like a commodity. They are people.

The first thing I set out to do was give the players a lot more power and say. I began to make a lot more decisions through group consensus rather that dictating everything myself. I think the players want and need to have a greater say over things that affect them. Not all things were up for debate, of course; I had to let them know that I was still a leader. Anything that dealt with our style of play or how we play, however, was very much up for debate. I had try to walk a fine line between my two roles.

Giving the players more ownership changed the relationship between the organization and the guys — it became much less an "us-them" mentality and much more like a family. And that change brought us closer together. As I player, I always wanted to be a more involved in this way, but my coaches would never let me have any input. With me in charge, things would be different.

The next big change I made was to establish a kind of players board of directors. David Robinson became president of our organization, Sean Elliott, Dale Ellis, and, later, Terry Cummings were vice presidents. I wanted to have these guys more involved in the day-to-day running of the team. They would either make or be very involved in decisions about travel, trades, and team discipline.

We talked about these things right away, but I'm not sure they really believed that I meant what I said. Soon enough they did! Before we left on the first road trip, I was sitting there on the plane, and the guys said, "You let us know when we have to go." I said, "Me?" They said, "Yeah, the coach decides when we leave." I said, "Well, you'd better ask David, because he sets the time for when we travel." They were pretty shocked.

Next I told the team that David would be setting the fines for the players. They said, "What! What do you mean David's going to set the fines?" They'd never seen anything like this before. Not much later, Dale missed a flight to Detroit and so David set the fine for Dale. We have what we call shoot-arounds in practice, and sometimes they're a contest. I promised the players that fine money would go to the winners of the shoot-arounds. I held true to my word, and the next day the money from Dale's fine went on the wood for the winners. The idea for this came from my experience with peer relationships and peer counseling.

All of this truly did give the players a feeling of ownership in the team. For as long as I'd been in basketball, there had been a feeling of players against management. What I wanted was a family environment — and that meant changes on the management side, too. At first, for example, Bob Bass wouldn't come into the locker room. And I said, "B. B., you can *always* come in the locker room. You are my boss. I want you to know this team. You've been in basketball for years. You can give input to everybody. Don't separate yourself." So B. B. was around a lot, and so was Bob Coleman, one of the owners. He and Pat, his wife, traveled all the time with us on the charter. Everyone felt more comfortable with each other.

One thing that I learned in recovery was to place principles before personalities. Players all have different personalities, and I put in place the principle of letting people be who they are to help them learn to love themselves — just as I would've wanted someone to do for me.

David Robinson

When I came into the league, this is what I expected. I always saw Magic and Bird, and knew they had a leadership role on their clubs. That's the way it ought to be, but when I joined the Spurs, it wasn't. The veterans were just kind of out there playing. They were good players, but they weren't doing anything with leadership; it was mainly the coach.

John realizes that the players are more intelligent than people give them credit for, and he tries to play into that. If you have good players, they know what's going on on the court. They see a lot more things and they can give some good feedback. I think, too, that this league is very different from the college level in that the players need to feel a part of the ownership. They need to play a bigger role than just going out there and playing. We are the game. You can put guys on the floor, but that doesn't ensure you're going to win with them. John really brings this out. He knows what we have to offer because he was a player. His attitude is, "Let's talk to them and see what they have to offer."

John's the first coach I've had who really let me be who I am. I've always wanted to be involved, but no one was interested in what I had to say. Once I had someone I could talk to, I think he got more production out of me in every area. It felt much more natural. That's the way it is supposed to be.

Dale Ellis

When he came in, John designated David and Sean Elliott and me to be a kind of spokesmen for the team. We had a role to play. We were part of what was going on. He really wanted to know what we thought. That was the first time I ever experienced something like that in my NBA career — or in my whole career. It was a real change. It shouldn't have seemed so strange, but it did. We're all adults, we're all professionals. We expect to go out and do our jobs, and we should be a part of what's going on, too.

With three days off before our next game, I had a little time to get my ideas out to the team. The first thing I did was to talk to them all as a group. I told them that they were out of shape, really out of shape, and that we were going to remedy that problem immediately. I said that I was learning the game, that they would learn with me, and that we would continue to grow together. I told them that their biggest problem was they didn't believe in themselves anymore, that we had a team that could win, and that we didn't need anyone else to do that. "We can win some games," I said, "more than you think. But to do that I need you all to help me. We need to work together. We're embarking on something new, so let's go out and have some fun."

After two days of practice, just before our first game, David came to me and said he wanted to talk. Now I thought we were going to be in this big meeting because maybe I was pushing them too hard or something, but he said, "You know, I don't talk a whole lot, but I would like to tell you that I think that what you're doing is moving us in the right direction. I just want to tell you I like what I see." Needless to say, hearing that from David gave me a big boost. I was on the right track.

We began to get into shape, and then went out to play our first game, which was against Denver. We played well and we won. Lloyd Daniels had pretty much been calling shots on this team, and at half-time, Lloyd was arguing because everybody had played but him. I said to him, "Lloyd, you don't have any rights here. You're just a rookie and you ain't never played no pro ball, so you got to shut up and listen and learn." And I remember David going, "Thank you, thank you." It wasn't that I said anything harsh. I think Lloyd thought that because we were both in recovery, I owed him something. That's true, but what I owe him isn't a chance to start, or even to play pro ball. What I owe him is a chance to keep living.

We headed to the Coast next to play the Clippers and the Lakers. We met the Clippers on Christmas Day on national TV. It's my second game coaching and we're on national TV! David had a great game and all the guys played really well. We beat the Clippers and, a couple days later, the Lakers as well. Our guys were beginning to believe in themselves, and they began to believe that I knew what I was doing.

Then our assistant coaches wanted to have a meeting with me. They were nervous. They expected that I would fire them and bring in my own guys because, I guess, that's what new coaches do. I wasn't into that. I wasn't about to fire anybody — or hire someone I didn't know — without interviewing people who were already there and without at least giving them a fair opportunity to show what they could do. My father taught me not to shortchange the people you already have. You can learn a lot from every person you meet; you just have to be willing to listen.

I was looking at the bigger picture anyway — we had to get a team in order. I told our coaches when I first took over that our players came first, that I believed in the power of players. I told them that as a player, I never felt that my coaches listened to the guys — so I'm going to empower our players. I said I didn't have time for meetings — let's just get the work done. So we settled everything. They saw that my style was going to be very different, that I wasn't trying to run a dictatorship, that I was very much open to input and very much liked to have fun — and they were in agreement with all of that. I like hard work, but it doesn't mean that it has to be dreary. The assistant coaches had a lot of input with me, and they've done a great job.

The one coaching change I did make when I came in was to get George Gervin for my chemistry coach. Gervin, the greatest Spur of all time, was doing marketing for the club. There's nothing wrong with that, but I thought he could have another role. I've always felt that you need a chemistry coach — a guy who could be a buffer between you and the players. Ice was perfect for the part: the players respected what he did as a player, he knew the game inside and out, and he had people skills.

I went after Ice right away. The day after I got the job, we were all practicing, and Ice was sitting in the stands watching us with Red McCombs. Partway through practice, I yelled up to him. I said, "Hey, Ice! I want you down here on the floor with me tomorrow. I want you to be my assistant coach. Get some gear and be dressed out tomorrow."

George sat there for a moment with his mouth open, and then he said, "What?" He didn't believe me, so he called me up that night, and said "What were you talking about today in practice? What do you want me to do?" I said, "I want you to be an assistant coach. We got a lot we can teach the guys."

George thought I was playing with his mind, but I wasn't. We got him out of his many obligations to the marketing department, and he became my coach. Then, in our first game as coaches, suddenly two guys are going at each other. I hear this "F you, F you, F you." They were arguing over a play that was called. I looked to see what the coaches were doing, and there's George saying, "Now fellows, fellows, fellows. Settle down, settle down." He was handling it.

Every time people have problems or feel they have a lack of playing time, Ice will talk to them and help them understand where I am coming from. You need a guy like Ice because nobody's going to like the coach all the time. I also feel very strongly that as an organization, we must continue to find places for the players that have done a lot for our city and our organization over the years. We have to give back, and I thought that this was the place where George needed to work and where he would be good for us.

Cheryl Lucas

One thing I really like about what John is trying to do, and that most people seem to miss, is that he has tried to give the players a feeling that they are more than just pieces of property. These guys have taken a true interest in what they're doing because John is someone who finally came along and said, "Okay, we pay a lot of money for you, and yes, you have to come to practice, and yes, you have to make games, and yes, you have to make the plane, but still, how do you feel about the team? What do you think we should be doing?" Those guys have to come there and risk their health every night. They should at least have something to say about what's going on. I really respect John for doing this because for a lot of athletes, and black athletes in particular, professional sports results in their selling their souls to get endorsements, to get a new contract, or whatever.

The players should be able to have some input in whatever they're doing. It doesn't need to be only about money. This is their job. Just because it happens to be basketball doesn't mean it's thoughtless. The players still have to think. They still have to make decisions. They still have to deal with the result of winning or losing. And it's a life experience — it's their life. Too often, nobody cares about athletes except for how much money can make off of them.

This gets to the essence of what John really is about. He's a real person who cares about other people — not about success or notoriety. John has actually gone through all of this and has realized that what it comes down to in the long run is to be the best that you can be — and he has convinced everybody else to try to do the same. Now if someone doesn't want to do that, that's fine. But if you're going to be a part of what he's about and what he's trying to do, then he wants you to get involved in this attitude. Why should John have to tell them what to do all the time when it's their team, too? When you have some responsibility for things, then it's a completely different deal. You're not merely somebody's pawn.

Another thing that John does that I really like is that he accepts people the way they are. He's not someone who'll come in and try to change everything. John tries to find what's good about each guy and then find a way to bring that out. David is a case in point. John has allowed David to play facing the basket more, and no one else has ever done that. I'm sure probably a lot of that came from David; David said himself he played the other way because people told him to and he never had anything to say about it. But when you can have some give and take, it makes a big difference. Look what David's doing now. John is learning a lot from the guys.

When I came in, the team had a 9-11 record. After I came, we began to set our own structure, and we won eighteen out of nineteen games. The players really came together. I think they thought what I was doing was refreshing. They had a lot of input and a lot of say. This can be a wild bunch at times. We don't have a lot of hard and fast rules, and we keep things pretty loose, but what appears to be chaos is, in fact, very structured.

I was having a real good feeling about being with San Antonio. The Rockets and San Antonio Spurs had long been the two organizations I really had a love for. As I said, were it not for the NBA-ABA merger, I would have probably become a Spur in 1976. I've always had a link to San Antonio and to Houston. Nothing came before the San Antonio Spurs, however, simply because Bob Bass got me off that bus and gave me a chance. So I had a strong loyalty to him and the Spurs organization. Coming back to coach the Spurs gave me a strong sense of coming home.

So I'm coaching, we are winning games, and all of a sudden the guys on the floor really began to believe in their abilities. I started to see a sense of pride come out. We made some lineup changes and started Avery Johnson. I tried to give everybody a chance to show what they could do, and we began to believe in each other.

I learned a lot from my high school coach, Carl Easterling, that I still apply today in my life. One thing is that my players have rights. I let them contribute. He used to say, "You show me what you think might work." It was like he was saying, "Here's the canvas, here's the paint brush, paint me a picture. Show me what you can do, and then I'll see if I can help you here or there. I'll point out some things." That's what I was trying to do. I let them show me what they could do.

I don't dwell on a person's weaknesses. I focus on their strengths. I try to create an environment in which players feel comfortable, and I give them some freedom to work within that environment. And I don't play games. All coaching is, is working with people, and I try to communicate through laughter and through love. It's like being a father or a mother. Really, I think I'm more a counselor than a coach.

David Robinson

What I respect most about John is that he really cares about us and he cares about what he's doing. He doesn't like to lose anytime, but I think it hurts him in a different way when we lose because we haven't given ourselves a chance. I think that's obvious to all the guys. It's special. There's a funny thing about motivation: if you say it right or do it right, some of the most simple things can work.

Dale Ellis

Compared to other coaches, John was great at listening to us. He had played, so he knew NBA basketball, but he didn't know all the guys in the league that well because he hadn't been close to it for a while. So we talked a lot as a team about strategies for games and about how to use different guys.

We began doing well because he made us feel like we were really a part of things. We were able to make decisions. We were a team. We were winning, and it wasn't just one guy telling us what we were going to do. We all had a say, and that really made us want to work hard, to play hard, and to respect each other. We really went out to win for him.

I've played with coaches who are dictators, and they say, "This is how it's going to be, and if you don't do it, then this is what's going to happen." They expect everyone to toe the same line.

But everybody has their own identity, their own person- ality, and Lucas could really deal with personalities. He knew that guys have their mood swings, so he'd take a little mouthing off from them, but we all respected him and we paid attention when he'd speak up and say I want this or I want that done. He treated us like adults, like professionals. He expected us to be professionals. We are professionals — we know we have to do that, and we do. You don't come late for practice if you're a true professional, you just know that. So Lucas was great in that sense. We were all individuals, but we all had one common goal — to win. John helped play- ers focus on what they needed to do, while at the same time, he treated everybody a little bit differently.

Luke had another advantage — he'd played the game. And he was a good player. Because he was a player, he knew all the tricks the guys pull, and he'd remind you and joke about it. So you couldn't fool him. He knew your ability and he expected you to go out and do your job every night, and if you didn't, you heard from him. He was truly a profes- sional.

We won our first three games, lost one, and then took the next eigh- teen. We went into the All-Star break at 34-14, good enough for first place in the conference. Everybody was saying that we were just on a honeymoon, but you don't win eighteen out of nineteen games and call it a honeymoon.

Another thing that I saw happening for me — especially in the first few games, though it continued that whole season, too — was that lots of NBA fans who were recovering addicts approached me on the bench before games to shake my hand or to simply pat me on the back. During the playing of the national anthem, I would see nods, winks, and waves from anonymous faces in the crowd. These things gave me a great deal of hope. I said to myself then, Whether I fail or make it as a coach, I will at least let other people like me know that I believe in miracles — because I am one.

David DuPree

I've seen something in John that I don't think many guys have seen. After he graduated from Maryland, John kept in touch with a lot of the ballplayers who grew up or played back East. Lots of them, including John, would come back to play in the off-season in the summer leagues with other pro players. I can tell you, there was some damn good ball played around there in the summer — some of those teams could have beaten some NBA teams. They'd play each other all summer.

Now this was pickup ball, and you know when you go to a playground and just pick teams, the guys usually argue for forty minutes over who's going to be on their team. Nobody wants to lose. But Lucas, hell, he would take anybody. He didn't care who was on his team. And here's the thing: I never saw the guy lose a pickup game.

John Lucas was the most dominant pickup basketball player I've ever seen. He would take guys who could hardly stand up, and they'd be making a lay-ups when they played for Lucas. John's mouth was running the whole time. You're distracted, he's talking trash; you're upset, he's laughing. And in the meantime, he's either shooting or feeding people

*and calling the shots. He was the only guy I'd ever seen on
the playground who didn't care who he played with. He
didn't care because he knew he was the man. He would play
with guys who weren't that good and he'd say, "You're playing with me, and I'm the man." You knew you were going to
be better; you didn't worry, you just went out there and won
with him.*

*People always asked the Rockets, "Why would you take
John Lucas first pick when there were so many other guys
you could have had?" Why? Because Lucas could control
the game, and he could really get people to overachieve —
and that's because they would believe in him. You cannot not
believe in John Lucas. It doesn't surprise me a bit what he
did with San Antonio. He's been doing it all his life as a player
— the only difference now is that he's just not on the floor.*

*John is something, and I'm a believer in him right now.
My father was an alcoholic who went through treatment after
treatment but never got sober. I grew up with the firm belief
that once you touched drugs, you were through. I believed
that it was absolutely impossible for you to beat it. No excep-
tions. And Lucas really changed my mind on that; he's gotten me to believe that it's possible to change your life. John
doesn't hide from his past, and he doesn't preach, either,
which I think is another thing that's great about him. He just
lives his life and you take what you can from it.*

We sent two guys to the All-Star game — David Robinson and Sean
Elliott, who we later traded to get Dennis Rodman. Elliott injured his
back in the game, and he missed seven games before he got himself
healthy and playing again. Our second half of the year wasn't so good,
but Elliott's injury wasn't the only reason why we lost games.

What happened next to us was something that I simply did not
anticipate. Our team had become very close, but then we became
scared of success. One of the things that happens to pro ballplayers in

particular is this: we are *very* competitive, and we never know when to shut if off. Guys began to try to expand their role rather than stay within it. Nothing was broke, but we were trying to fix it anyway. We tampered with a good thing, and we ended up losing ourselves.

Also, everyone got a little selfish. Everybody was getting their share of success on the floor, and they all wanted to be rewarded financially. Greed set in on our team. Guys were trying to jockey themselves and expand their roles to get more money. The one thing that I had to get rid of to get sober and to stay sober was my ego. Now we had a lot of ego on our team — people looking at extended contracts and whatever.

Once egos got involved, people began to complain. So one day in Cleveland, I had group therapy with them. I brought everybody into the room and made everybody share something that was on their mind. I found out that one of the coaches who was around before I took over had told one guy that another guy wanted him traded. Turns out, that wasn't the case, and we were able to clean that up. Things like this — holding grudges — are really bad for a team. I tell the players all the time, "You can't have any secrets. If you've got a problem with one another, let's get it resolved."

Other stuff came out, too. Some of the guys who had played a lot couldn't believe I'd changed the lineup, and they thought I had lost confidence in them. We had also started passing the buck, and losing will do that. I told them that the best way to test your character is when things aren't going well.

After everyone had had a chance to speak at the meeting, I summed things up. I said, "Now I've got coaches who can't get along, I've got players who are fighting against one another, I've got wives who think their husbands should be playing, and so on and so on." I told them I had to take some ownership in all of this, too. I think that teams found out what we were doing and exposed our weaknesses. As a young coach, maybe I didn't make the proper adjustments that we needed, or perhaps what I did, I didn't do soon enough — or maybe we just plain didn't play well. Probably it was a combination of all of it.

Then I said, "So now let me tell you what we're going to do. We're going to get through this year, we're going to come back together, we're going to find a way to win, and we're going to see if we can get fifty wins this year."

I think coaching is as much people skills as it is X's and O's and the technical aspects of the game. If you can sell an idea to your players and they're willing to do it for the betterment of the whole team, then you've accomplished a lot — and I think there's a lot of different ways to get to that.

And, most importantly, I think my players know as much basketball as I do, and I need to listen. All my coaches put the players first, like I do. They work as hard as I do for the betterment of the players.

David DuPree

John could always relate to people, and he was honest — he would take responsibility when he'd make a mistake. I've covered the NBA through Bird, Michael, and Magic, and John Lucas is the only player I can remember covering who could criticize a teammate in such a way that it really wasn't a criticism. He could tell you why his team lost the game, that it would be a certain player's fault, but the way he would say it would make it come across as if it really wasn't that person's fault. He could cover for his teammates without lying. John had a remarkable way about him with this, and that's why I knew he could be a good coach.

If you think about this, you can understand why players really like playing for him. From what I hear, that seems to be part of the reason they can handle his being straight with them. He doesn't put anybody down, yet he can be tough when he needs to be.

David Robinson

One of the strongest things about John is that he's a confronter. He won't run from a problem. If you've got one, he wants to hear about it. He wants to get in there and mix it up.

I'm a confronter-type person, too. I don't like any hidden secrets, man. I don't like any animosity I don't know about. I'd rather you tell me what's bothering you, and then we can have it out right there. When you get everything worked out like that, everything is clean and pure. You work together and it's great. But if you have the murmurs and whispers, every-thing is poisoned. So John has a lot of those kind of sessions. When we're struggling, he'll have everybody sit down and just start talking about what's on people's minds and what's in their hearts.

We pushed on with our troubles, and it took until the end of the sea-son to get our egos checked and our faith in ourselves back. We went something like fourteen and eighteen the second half of the season and ended up in fifth place for the playoffs. We beat Houston the last reg-ular season game on a last-second tip that could have been called either way — and that victory seemed to carry us on a positive note into the playoffs, and we just kept right on going.

The Spurs hadn't gotten out of the first round of playoffs for four years. We had a very good basketball team that year — we ended up winning forty-nine games in the regular season, which was better than we thought we were going to do. But we were still bickering; we'd lost the harmony we'd been playing with in the first half of the season. And we were scheduled to play Portland in the first round — the Blazers were a good team.

We had a week off before the first game, so I took our team away to San Marcos for a little retreat. Just the guys. No family, no wives. Away from the city. Away from everybody. We all had single rooms in a hotel, and it was a great place to be — quiet, relaxing. I took us all to a movie together; we all rode buses together to practice. We practiced twice a day, we worked on our offense, and we began to come together.

After a great practice week, we left for Portland. I thought we were playing the best basketball of our lives, but we opened up our first game and we were awful. We were very tight, very tentative, but at the end of the game we a got chance for a last shot to win, and we made it. We won the second game, too, but this time we played well. We came back home and lost the third game. The fourth started off strangely, but not because of basketball. We had a tremendous storm and they had to move the game back half an hour because of flooding. We were down and ready to get beat in that game, but we came back. We were down something like ten points with four minutes to go, and it looked like Portland was going to take it back to Portland and have a fifth game. I told the team, "Refuse to lose, refuse to lose." And we came back enough to get back in the game. David hit the winning play, a shot that put us in the position to win, and then we played good defense to keep it, and so we beat Portland in the first round of the playoffs. Now Portland had beat San Antonio in a very exciting series four years previously, one that our organization thought we should have won, so this was a great win.

I really felt that this was a major accomplishment for our team because we had gone from not even thinking about the playoffs, to making the playoffs, to being a first-round winner — something the Spurs hadn't done in four years.

In the second round we played Phoenix. We opened up the first two games trying to play them with a slow-down game. We'd seen the Los Angeles Lakers do that very successfully against them with a big lineup and just jamming the ball inside, and we thought it might work for us, too.

But it didn't. We got killed. We weren't really even in those games — and that's because we weren't playing the style that had gotten us where we were. We tried to take on a personality that wasn't us. Then I said to myself, *The principles of recovery tell me to be who I am*, so I came into our meeting and said, "You know, guys, we're going to go back to pushing the ball up and down the floor. We're going to be ourselves. We're going to play our game. We're going to come out, we're going to push the ball up hard, and we're going to attack." That's what we did, and we won the next two games.

But then I forgot for a moment who I was. I could see the possibility here — two more victories, and who knows, maybe an NBA title.

This year. Now. We get it all. I became just another coach — more demanding, meaner. I hurt people verbally. I was less forgiving. We had gotten further than I anticipated, but I was getting upset. So much so that David pulled me aside and told me I better back off. And I did. I had to catch myself. I couldn't let my purpose for being here change.

So now the series was 2-2, and we went back to Phoenix. Going into game five, however, we knew we'd be playing without Antoine Carr because he'd turned an ankle in game four. It was a big loss because he'd been doing such a great job guarding Charles Barkley. We pushed the ball up there, too, and had a good game. We were beating them all the way through three quarters, but we couldn't pull it out. Now we were down 3-2. Entering the fourth quarter of the sixth game, we were up ten points to start the fourth quarter. They came back, caught us and went ahead, and then we caught back up. With eighteen seconds to go, they called time out. They had the last play again. I put David on Charles Barkley — two All-Stars going against each other — but Charles hit the winning shot and put us out.

We had a good year. A very good year. We came back from injuries to key players — David's knee and Sean's back. We went a lot further than we had hoped to go. I felt we still would have been playing if we hadn't lost Antoine. We were a very good team, both individually and collectively. As great a player as David is, one guy can't get it done by himself.

As a coach, I made some mistakes, like getting too carried away in the playoffs. Another had to do with making promises I couldn't keep. Earlier in the season when we were in Chicago, we were struggling a little and I knew some of the guys were thinking about their money. I said to one of them, "Don't worry about it, I'll see to it that you get your contract. Stop worrying about money." But in the end, his role changed for our team and we decided not to bring him back. The guys remembered that. They remembered I'd told a guy he'd be back, and then we didn't sign him. That was a big mistake because you never know what tomorrow holds. Certainly I wasn't lying to him, and my intentions were to bring him back, but as we got into the second round of the playoffs, I thought that our team needed to move in another direction.

There were several guys on the team I knew very well — Larry Smith and Avery Johnson — and I had to tell them they weren't going to be able to come back. They were two of my closest friends, and close friends of my family, too. That was very hard for me. I'll be happy when I don't have that kind of tie to my players anymore. It's too hard.

Bob Bass

We had a good team to start with, but John fit with them so well that with the things he did, well, it just took off. The enthusiasm was there, the competitiveness was there, and we won some big games against good teams. It really went well until the All-Star break. We hit a snag then and didn't play real well for the rest of the season until we got in the playoffs. Then we beat Portland in the playoffs, and took Phoenix to six before going out. We had a real good shot until Antoine got hurt.

You could tell by just being in the locker room what the players thought about John. Of course every player wants minutes, and the ones who don't get them are usually unhappy. But John did a great job with that in trying to keep those guys from completely losing their interest. What's more, John is just very good with people. He's a communicator. He let the players contribute. John had the final say on everything but he also made them part of it. His players feel like it's their team, too.

John was very inexperienced but he's really made some giant strides as a coach. John's becoming a real student of the game just like any dedicated coach does.

I was very much looking forward to the 1993-94 season. Coming to a team midseason, like I did my first year with the Spurs, always puts a coach in a more difficult position, especially if you're new to NBA coaching. While I was very pleased with how we did in 1992-93, I was glad to have the chance to take the club from start to finish.

I did feel, however, that we needed to make some changes to improve our team so we could continue to compete with the good teams in the Western Division. Seattle, Portland, Phoenix, Houston, and Utah were all doing things to help themselves, and Bob Bass and I knew we couldn't stand pat, either. We knew we needed someone who could do the inside work — pulling down rebounds and playing tough defense — so David Robinson could be freed up to go out on the floor where he could face the basket and make better use of his talents. I looked at other clubs and saw that nearly every big guy had someone help out this way — Patrick Ewing had Charles Oakley, and Hakeem had Otis Thorpe.

Wanting to make a trade is one thing; finding the right guy who's also available is another. And we did. Dennis Rodman wanted to leave Detroit, so we traded Sean Elliott to acquire Dennis. This trade was clearly one great player going for another one, and it brought two very different reactions. Inside basketball, there was near-universal agreement that Dennis could be a tremendous help to David and the Spurs, provided we could work with him. Dennis was a tremendous rebounder, and he had been voted the league's best defensive player a couple years back. Sure, Dennis was a little bit different, had his own ideas about things, and had some history coming from Detroit. Still, I had no doubt that he could fit in here and help us. Among the media in San Antonio, however, the trade was neither well appreciated nor well understood. Sean Elliott was very well liked in the community, and a lot of people hated to see him leave. What's more, when people looked at Dennis, all they saw was his reputation. They felt we were getting a bad guy, a troublemaker.

When I got sober, I dropped a lot of prejudices I used to have toward people. I learned to look deeper to find out more about who a person *really* is rather than base my opinion about them on what they do or wear. Before Dennis came to the Spurs, I told people I didn't know what had been done to him in Detroit, but I was going to see what I could undo. Dennis is first of all a person, and a beautiful person at that, but he'd been robbed of his personhood by people he played with, his coaches, and the press. They depicted him as someone with all these mental problems. Sure he did have some problems his last year in Detroit, but I think more than anything he just wanted to get out of Detroit. You can find guys all over the league who don't like their situation and who are having trouble in their hometowns as a result.

As we started into my second year with the Spurs, I could see that I had changed as a coach. I was more decisive about what I wanted to do on the bench. I was more knowledgeable about timing and about the technical aspects of the game. I hadn't done a bad job my first season, but I really didn't think I handled myself as well as I could have, and I wasn't as prepared as I wanted to be for the second half of the year. I could see right away that things would be different because I knew the strengths and weaknesses of my team right from the beginning. I understood their makeup and their personalities. That let me make better decisions about what plays to run, what type of defenses to run, how to substitute, and so on. Those were some of the intangibles that I didn't have as good a feel for my first year because I didn't know the guys well enough.

Bob Coleman

I think John Lucas is the finest young coach in the entire NBA. It was absolutely amazing to me to see the changes in John's coaching in the short time he'd been with the Spurs. He became much more confident, much more focused. The record speaks for itself. Look at what he accomplished his two years with the Spurs. I think John's coaching is just going to get better and better. Eventually we won't be talking about one of the best young coaches in the league, we'll be talking about the best coach in the league.

John's strength is that he realizes that he's still developing. John doesn't have so much ego that he won't listen to other experienced people and take advantage of their input.

I continued the policy I began the year before of keeping the guys involved in decision making and in running the team. Recovery has shown me how to step back and let others take a role. I've seen what groups can do, and I know that power is with people rather than in me trying to tell people what to do. In a sense, I've taken the Twelve Step meeting and put it in the team environment. This has given me the peace of mind to feel comfortable about admitting that maybe my way isn't the best way all the time. If I give the players an opportunity to grow, then I can grow, too.

I don't need to be a dictator to prove my authority; we all know who the coach is. I don't wear a shirt that says "Coach." I don't spend all my time in meeting rooms or press conferences; I'm out working with my players. And they know that for me, the players are first.

I'm part father figure, part counselor, part coach. I talk to my players more about their character than about basketball. I believe that if we have good character, we'll want to win games. I really try to convey to the players that basketball is what they do, it's not who they are. I want them to find out who they are, and I'm trying to help them use basketball as a tool to do that.

Dale Ellis

I'd been with the Spurs a while, and things really changed when John came. It became like more of a family with Lucas. You could actually sit down and talk to him about things that were important to you — about your life. A lot of coaches I have played for don't have that kind of personal relationship with their players. John was a strong person in a position of authority, but he cared about us as people, too. He wasn't all basketball.

Lucas really loved basketball and it was part of what he was doing, but he felt like he could teach us about other things, too. He'd made some mistakes and felt he could help other people avoid them. When we'd travel, on the plane or in the bus, he'd often talk about his experiences in basketball and about his life. He'd joke about things that most people would say were horrible experiences. I'm amazed at what he's able to laugh about now. What he's doing is remarkable. John knows what is important. The players were like his kids in a way, but he always knew we were grown adults. He'd offer advice, and if he saw a problem, he'd sit you down individually and talk to you about it if he thought it was going to cause trouble for you. It's just fantastic the way he can work with people. I loved playing for him.

Dennis, David, and my whole team were a delight to coach in the 1993-94 season. The rest of the players supported David — and that was a first for him in his pro career. They had a spirit among themselves that I hadn't felt with other teams I'd been associated with. We had quite a group of guys, some near the ends of their careers, and they all came together to become a very good basketball team. I love to listen to people and I love to find hoops they are willing to jump through for themselves. I think over the course of my time in San Antonio we all saw that there is more than one way to get to the same goal. My way may not be your way.

David Robinson

John knew I respected him and his position. I didn't try to infringe on his authority. It was nice to have that kind of rapport. We didn't battle for control like some people in our positions might have done. Both of us just wanted to win, and I think that's really the key — so it worked out. Another thing John liked was to stay out of the limelight, and I'm the same way. We complemented each other very well.

John is truly a learner, and I can tell you, it was very different to have a coach who was willing to say, "Yeah, I can learn from you guys too." A lot of players have been around for a long time; they've gone from team to team, and they've seen just about everything there is to see. They have a valuable perspective on the game and the league. This is a people game, and whether you like it or not, you'd better be a good manager of people. You got to be able to see what your guys can do and use them in a way they can be used. If you can't do that, no matter how much you know about basketball, you'll end up being frustrated. It's amazing that people don't take a more humble attitude when it comes to learning things. They just don't know so much. None of us do.

Everything John has lived through has become a part of him, and he doesn't try to hide anything. I think when a man gets crushed in his personal life, you usually get a different and better man. A lot of the things he's learned from drug rehab — the programs that he's been involved with and the people he's met — well, he brings this right along with him. It's obvious that that's a big part of his life — not just of his past. It's played a major and very positive role in shaping the way he looks at and feels with the world.

Amazingly, though, John doesn't seem preachy at all. I think mainly that's because he's still experiencing the struggle himself. He's in recovery. It's hard to preach to somebody when you know your own inadequacies. Everybody needs to know their own weaknesses. You have to feel your own mortality before you can really help somebody else, and I think John does. What's more, he doesn't dwell on them. He tries to go beyond them, and that's something I really appreciate and respect.

We went through a whole bunch of lineups, we went through a lot of things, but we were always looking toward tomorrow. We were always trying to figure out what's going to work tomorrow. It's hard not to dwell on the losses, the bad things, the weaknesses that you have, but John does a real good job of not doing that. He's a real upbeat person, and what this does is create a healing situation. He really believed that we could win with who we had in the locker room — and that's something we all came to believe — but it took us time to grow into that.

It's obvious that John just cares about us as people — as people who happen to play basketball. He always has time for people, and that shows in the way he coaches. John has a lot of passion, but he doesn't lose perspective very often, and that's probably one of his biggest strengths. He has a good sense for backing up to see the bigger picture — another reason the players can really respect him.

In my second season I really worked to help the guys develop the expectations and goals they needed — and wouldn't be willing to meet — to reach their own success. Not mine, theirs. While I also continued to let them monitor themselves, I took a firmer hand in my coaching role. But as far as their emotions go, I didn't have to do anything about that. They didn't need me. They were very motivated and emotionally into their games, and I think that that's because most of the guys were there from the year before. I worked had that first year to get them to understand that this was their team and they were going to be here for a while. The result is that they took more ownership in the team and its success or failure.

Tom Nissalke

All kinds of friends of mine were telling me his first year that John was not going to make it, that he was no coach. Speaking from my own experience, at the NBA level, X's and O's are the least important thing by far. Getting people to play hard every night and getting their respect — those are the most difficult things to deal with. John somehow managed to take one of the best players in the NBA — David Robinson — and get him to go to even another level. And then to bring in Dennis Rodman and get the play out of him that John got — it's unbelievable. What's more, John came into a very tough situation with very little experience, one where the expectations were high. Not only did he not miss a beat, he improved on their situation. That's not just admirable, it's amazing.

Just as there's no road map to recovery, there's no road map to coaching, either. I don't see myself so much as a coach as I do a person who can work with people. I just try to convey messages to my players in a way they understand so they can do it for themselves. You can be the best X and O guy, the best technical guy with the most knowledge of the game, but if the players don't want to do it, it won't get done. So I tell the newcomers, "If you want what we have, then there are certain steps you have to take to get it. Here's the outline, you build your own program."

What that means is that I try to create an environment conducive for learning. I set up a family atmosphere in which it's okay to experiment, an environment where people don't have to worry about what they say. I love the guys both on and off the court. I have a full commitment to them, and that means caring about them off the court, trying to show some love and compassion to issues in their lives not related to basketball.

I had a good time my second year. I liked that I had a group of guys who were very mixed — some conformists and others noncomformists. I liked the emotion they had, and I liked that they didn't always agree with me. I wanted them to play more as though the team was theirs, not mine, but it takes time to get to that point. I was just the manager. I could only help them so much. Another thing I liked about this team was that everybody was honest. I didn't have to guess what they were thinking. Dennis helped bring that out in everybody.

A lot has been written and said about Dennis Rodman, but there's been very little, if anything, that accurately describes why we traded for him or how it was to have him on the team.

Everybody thought that I wanted Dennis because my mission is to take on troubled people. That's simply not true. This was strictly a basketball decision. David Robinson needed someone to ride roughshod on the inside for him so we could get the best out of him, and we felt Dennis could do that. The result: David led the league in scoring with 29.8 points per game, and Dennis led the league in rebounding with 17.3 per game. That's the first time in NBA history that teammates have led the league in these two categories in the same year. In addition, Dennis brought a higher level of intensity and toughness to our team, and that's something we needed, too. Dennis had something we needed, but I think we had something he wanted and needed, too. Dennis wasn't very happy in Detroit his last few years there, and I wanted him to be happy about life again.

I thought taking Rodman was something of a risk, but not a big one. I felt that if I could talk to him about the hoops he was willing to jump through and the hoops I was willing to jump through, we could reach a common ground.

Dirk Minniefield

The players say John is a player's coach. The greatest gift you can give players in the NBA is to have another player coach them, because they feel he can understand them. I don't think there's a player in the whole league who wouldn't love to play for him.

Another thing about John is that with all the turmoil he's been through in his life and what he's done to get his life to where it is today, he looks at people entirely differently than anybody else I've known. John will recognize the bad in someone, but he'll always look for the good and see what he can do with it.

Some things that might be unacceptable to other people John can deal with. I think that comes from all his work on himself and working with other people who have drug problems. When you work with them, you are really put in touch with all kinds of problems. People are going to act in a lot of different ways, and the bottom line is whether a guy is willing to do what it takes to get the job done.

If he's willing and does get it done, those other things that were not so important will eventually fall into line. People begin to learn that certain behaviors are detrimental to them. That's the way John deals with people — he believes that it's about growth. That's why John can say, "Come on, come play for me. I can understand some things other people can't. I can see beyond the problem. We can get to a solution together. I'll work with you if you work with me."

When we got Dennis I felt that he and I were similar people in some ways. When Dennis played in Detroit, he was stuck behind a lot of other stars. We felt that playing for the Spurs would give him a chance to shine, to really use the huge talent he has.

When he arrived in San Antonio, Dennis told me he hoped there wasn't a dress code because he wasn't a big believer in suits and ties. I said to him, "Just keep your shoelaces tied." I also told him that his presence at shoot-arounds and pregame warm-ups would also be permanently optional. I had no desire to make Dennis conform, to try to fit him into a little box. As long as he does his job, I couldn't care less what color hair he has or what he wears. Because of all the work in recovery I've done, I'm willing to accept people for who they are and where they are — just as I hope they will accept me for who I am.

Of course we talked as a team about the trade and about Dennis. I told the guys I was going to allow Dennis more latitude in some areas than other people. Dennis is a different guy. He doesn't like to go to shoot-arounds. He's late for meetings or practices sometimes, too. No one had a problem with it. If the rest of the guys don't care, then we don't have a problem. From time to time during the season, I would check in to see if everyone still felt the same way, and they did.

I can tell you, too, that it didn't take anyone long to find out that even if they didn't always know what Dennis was going to do for twenty-one hours of the day, for those three hours that we were in the game, he was right there leading the charge. Dennis fit in very well. I didn't have any expectations about Dennis as a person before he came, and I told my team not to, either. We accepted him for who he is. For the most part, a guy everyone said was hard to deal with wasn't hard for us to work with.

Dale Ellis

A lot of coaches wouldn't want Dennis on their team. But John understood Dennis, and Dennis understood John. And as far as the rest of us, one guy wasn't worried about another guy getting away with something. Besides, when Dennis steps on the floor, he's all business and he gets the job done. What else do you want? He helped us bring it all together. If he or anybody is late for practice, well, we're professionals and we can't get involved in that kind of stuff. That's the coach's job.

The team and I had a love-hate relationship in a way. I was either yelling and hollering at Dennis, yelling and griping at David, or they were yelling and griping with me. But we all loved each other. It was all about trying to get to their best level of play.

Dennis Rodman

I didn't think about coming to the Spurs. They weren't my first option. But after a while, I thought it wouldn't be so bad. I looked at it and I said, "Whatever. I guess I'll go."

I hadn't heard much at all about Lucas. In a way, he's no different than any other coach, but he's pretty laid back. He can be intense when he needs to be, and that's when the great coaches come out. You need to be intense at the right time. Lucas wants to win — that's the best part of it — he wants to win, and you can see that. He's exuberant, too, and I'm hoping that he don't lose that.

Lucas has come a long way already, but he is still a young coach. He has a lot to learn, like how to manage himself so he can be involved, not so much in the play but in what he can do to help the team be a team. You can't coach and handle players like babies. You can't. You got to let them develop and be men. You've got to let them make their mistakes, and John's learning how to do that. Sometimes I think he's worried about hurting peoples feelings. You can't worry about that. You got to go out there and let the guys know where you're coming from.

John is trying to develop his own coaching style and have everybody believe in what he does. I believe in what he does, and the other guys believe, too. John spends a lot of time talking about character, about how to live life. That's the way to do it. I think before a player can go out on the court, he's got to fight the battle within himself. Once you do that, you can win a lot of battles, and then you can go out there and compete. I think Lucas tries to get that out of every player.

It seems that everybody wants you to be who they want, but John lets everybody be themselves, especially me. He don't press me. He knows he's going to get the best. He knows that if I'm not doing my job, he can tell me — and he will. But rarely does he say that to me because he knows I'm going to go out there and do it. He doesn't have to say, "Go out there and do something!"

People want to know if I'm happier in San Antonio than I was in Detroit. Well, it's hard to say, because when you first go somewhere, it's different, new, and vibrant. Everyone thinks it's exciting to be a team that's winning regularly. Well, not really. It's not the win that's the most important thing in life. What's important is this battle with all the distractions, the anxieties; the everyday constant battle of trying to deal with life itself. If you can do that, well, that's the battle you got to win. You got to try to deal with your own personal stuff and then the other things take care of themselves.

That's why sports is not the most important thing to me. It's an activity that can keep me busy. You got to be happy with yourself more than anything. You can't just go and do it for the money. Once you do that, everything that you believe in and what you are trying to accomplish will go down the drain. Happiness is the most important thing. Money isn't it. Money can get you everything in the world. It can buy you any car, any house, any thing in the world, but there's always something missing. Money can't buy happiness, I can tell you that. All it does is create more problems.

This pro ball business is nothing but a fantasy, that's all it is. It's like going to Fantasy Island and fulfilling all your dreams. But once you get out, it's like you're still living a dream but you don't have the applause, you don't have the cheers. All that is gone and everything is suddenly silent. Nobody knows who you are — you're a has been. All the people can do is say, "Remember, remember he made that great move fifteen years ago." I don't want to hear that crap.

I'm just trying to fill a part, that's all. It's no big deal. Playing the game is really stressful and it really gets to you. I get really tired, but I'll keep playing as long as my body holds out.

This team has totally turned around to become one of the best teams in the league and a lot of people are saying I'm the main reason we're doing so well. No, I'm just here doing a job. I don't really know why we turned around. It's like somebody once said, "You gotta let boys be men." You gotta let them grow up and sooner or later things start to happen.

David and Dennis had very good seasons individually, but more than that, we accomplished a lot together as a team. The fifty-five wins we had was just one shy of the all-time franchise record set in 1989-90. We set a franchise record with thirteen straight wins from January 22 to February 21, and in wins on the road with twenty-three. We had the second best mark in the NBA after Christmas, posting a 40-16 record from that point on. We finished second to the New York Knicks in scoring defense, allowing 94.8 points per game. The club drew a total of 1,009,755 fans for the 1993-94 season, and finished second in the NBA in regular season attendance. It was a great year.

The postseason was, however, another story. We ended up in the toughest of the two brackets, where we faced Utah, a team who gave us so much trouble this year that we never defeated them in the regular season. We did very well in the first game and won by about twenty points. But that was all we would be able to do.

We had hit a slump at the end of the season. Dale Ellis got hurt, and we won only two of our last nine games. He was able to play against the Jazz, but he wasn't himself. Then we lost Dennis for a game, due to a suspension for a flagrant foul, and we ended up losing the series in four games. We were very disappointed by this loss, especially after such a successful regular season.

This loss brought out one of the hard things about coaching for me. As a new coach, I'm learning on the job, and it's like doing a Fourth Step in a Twelve Step AA program (a fearless and searching moral inventory) after every game — you have to defend your decisions and explain yourself all the time. It's very public. The media question you after every game, but after our playoff loss to the Jazz, they just ripped us. *Everything* came under a very intense scrutiny. They didn't let up. All the stuff about the Rodman trade was resurrected again, and no one was noticing or mentioning anything about all we had accomplished in the regular season.

In the light of all the criticism, I felt that I almost had to apologize for what both I and the team had done the whole year. Whenever you make a trade, it's a business decision. But it also involves people, and you don't every really know how it will work out. You just have to hope for the best. I still think this was a good trade. I was trying to add a piece to the team that would help us win more games. And it clearly did. We won six more games than last year, only one short of the franchise record. As a coach, I've averaged fifty-three wins a year, and that's the best record over two years in the league for a new young coach.

I was upset and disappointed about our first round loss, too, but I felt that our season needed to end anyway. We could have gone on, but I think if we had, it would have continued to tear down what we were trying to build. I think what happened was this: David received a lot of accolades this year, and Dennis did, too. As a result, the whole team was in the spotlight more — and eventually, basketball became secondary. The main show was Dennis and David. I think some of the guys took offense that David was being talked about for the MVP. And Dennis, well, he was being Dennis. As a result, he got a lot of attention, and that was hard for some people.

The arrival of Dennis Rodman in San Antonio created a kind of culture shock for this town. This is a very conservative and very military town. Within the league, a lot of people said it was the best trade we could ever have made. The local media, however, didn't like it, but not for basketball reasons. Here's a guy who's a little wild, he gets thrown out of some games, he takes his shirt off on the sidelines, he flips people off sometimes. Well, they don't like that stuff in San Antonio. It's too East Coast.

Things changed enormously for Dennis during the year — he became a big star. When he was with Detroit, he was a star among stars, but here he became the number-two guy and a superstar. He started getting a lot more publicity than he had ever before. I don't think Dennis either expected this or knew how to handle it when it happened. I think all the publicity Dennis was getting began to wear on our team. And when he became very popular with the fans — which he is now — some people had a hard time understanding that, particularly in the local media and maybe even among some of the Spur management.

Complicating matters for him even more, Dennis was getting very mixed messages in another way. Dennis gets really wound up before a game, and when he hits that court, he's in another zone. We need that intensity — we want good, clean, hard, aggressive place. Toward the end of the season and in the playoffs, Dennis was called for some flagrant fouls, and neither I nor the league will tolerate that kind of play. But while the league didn't like some of what Dennis was doing on the court and even fining and suspending him for it, the fans were loving it. I don't think Dennis knew exactly how to react to that. Should he react to fans or to the league? Who is he really playing for?

I very much still believe in Dennis Rodman. He gives so much effort when he plays, more than any player I've been around. He was great for us this year, and he's just going to get better. I know, too, that I could have done a better job with him to build discipline on the court. Dennis does not have an off-court problem. It's an on-court problem. He got suspended a couple times at the end of the season, so he needs to learn how to avoid that. Because of the intensity and emotion he plays the game with, I know he will still draw some technicals. Nobody should try to remove that emotion; it's very much a part of who he is. But he can't help the team if he isn't on the floor.

Dennis will have to learn that pro basketball has become a marketing tool through which some people are making a tremendous amount of money. These people are not going to tolerate a bad-boy image on the court. Dennis can still be something of an irritant, but not so much that it's a detriment to the team by its losing him. I tried to treat him with a lot of love — as consistent with how I live my life.

Dennis and some of the rest of the guys need to remember that they don't just represent themselves when they play, especially in San Antonio. People there see the team as representing them and their city, so the guys will have to remember that when they put on a Spurs uniform. Today some athletes are not into being role models. They say they are just being paid to do a service. Well that's a nice idea, but the reality is that they are role models — whether they want to be or not. As a result, they have a public responsibility. Just as I've been saying all along, I'm in a similar position. Because I'm in recovery, I am a role model for recovery — whether I want to be or not.

One of my goals when I went to the Spurs was to get them back to a high level again. And we did that. We got the scoring title back, and we got the rebounding title back. The last piece, of course, would have been to win a championship, and I think we'd have had a shot at that. We won fifty-five games in the 1993-94 season, but finished fourth in our conference. I think we needed a couple things to make ourselves a little better, but we were in a tough conference. I don't think we could have done much better than fifty-five games. As a coach, you can't do much about how your team reacts to the stresses of the long season. NBA basketball is very public, and outside influences are going to make themselves felt. You just have to hope your players are mature enough to handle it, but toward the end of the season we weren't. We were distracted. We needed to get the focus back on the basketball court and on our team. The further we'd have gone in the playoffs, the further astray that focus would have gotten. It's just such a different situation, and there are a lot of things no one can control.

For about ten days right after the 1993-94 season ended, I was by no means sure that the Spurs wanted me around anymore. The media were relentless in their criticism of us. Then the team's board and the rest of the owners got involved. Everyone was really down on the Rodman trade, and on Bob Bass for making the deal. After all we had accomplished, I couldn't believe what was happening.

Suddenly, I was in the middle of more challenge and adversity. I can tell you, it was a very difficult ten days. No one knew who's job was safe. I was assured that mine was, but anyone who has even a casual interest in sports knows that many a manager and coach have been fired days or even hours after such assurances have been made by owners. A lot of emotions came up for me. I wondered what I should do. And resigning crossed my mind early on. Then, Bob Coleman, president and CEO of the club resigned his position under pressure, and Bob Bass, a man I deeply respect both as a basketball guy and as a person, a man who helped me very much in my life, was fired from his position as head of basketball operations.

That week while the owners group was deciding what action to take was not a pleasant time. Everything that was said in the board meetings became public knowledge. A lot of negative things were said about Bob Bass, Bob Coleman, me, and the team, and it was all over the papers. Ridiculous things like "Lucas jumps around too much on the sidelines when he's coaching."

I don't want to let it be said that I have thin skin as far as the media goes. We did lose in the first round of the playoffs. Our players were upset, and of course the coach has to expect to take the brunt of the criticism. And I'm the first to admit that I made some mistakes and would have done some things differently next season. That didn't bother me. People have a right to say what they want, but I just hated the idea that they let it all get out of the boardroom. I had been giving my heart and soul to that team — and to the city of San Antonio. I'd made coaching the Spus a twenty-four-hours-a-day job. I tried to be there for the players when they needed me in their personal lives, too. It was more than a job to me, and it really hurt to hear what the people I worked for were saying about me. There was no acknowledgement of my contributions, either.

I really loved San Antonio, but after Bob Bass was fired, I really began to question whether I could in conscience continue with the organization. With me as a coach, we won fifty-five games, but we couldn't have done that without the help of Bob Coleman and Bob Bass. Both men stood up for me, and look what happened to them. Management can do whatever they want. I understand that. But Bob Bass had a right to leave the Spurs in a way that took into account all that he had give to and done for that organization in his twenty-two years of service to them. Instead he was fired with hardly a thank-you — and after he helped the team to the second-best record in franchise history.

Next, management began bringing in a number of their own people — guys that they had been planning to hire. That was fine, too. I think whenever you come in, you want to bring in your own people and sweep the slate clean. I was never angry about that. But suddenly I realized I was the only one left.

I didn't want it to look like I was running out on my players, and I know that David Robinson, for one, was angry with me. But it wasn't about the players. They're a great basketball team, one that's on the verge of greatness. But I've been in basketball a long time, and I know how these things go. It's a business, and in this kind of situation, the next person's head in the guillotine would be mine — with the blade waiting only for some perceived indiscretion or failure on my part to release it.

When I met with the board, I was really asking for a concrete demonstration of their confidence in me, but I didn't get it. They felt I didn't have enough experience to be their general manager. They weren't willing to extend my contract or increase my responsibilities in any other way. They were willing to keep me as coach, but that was it. There was no room for growth. I feel that if I don't have the confidence of the people I'm working for, they should let me go. Don't let me wonder and be looking over my shoulder all the time. For my own health, emotions, and recovery, I felt I had to make a change. They had pretty much cleaned house already, and I realized that the best thing to do was to make a clean break of it.

Contrary to what some people have said, I didn't have another job in my back pocket before I left. My resignation was a leap of faith. I made sure I could take my coaches with me wherever I went. Ice (George Gervin) wanted to come, too, but I thought it would be better for him to stay with his family and closer to his son. I made certain that he would be able to stay with the organization. Ice has so much history there. Ice is the Spurs.

It was really great to get the offer from the Philadelphia 76ers so quickly after I resigned. The decision to go with them has turned out to be a tremendous opportunity for growth for me. With the 76ers, I'll be vice president for basketball operations, general manager, and coach.

I feel like I've been preparing for this for a very long time. I've run my own company for eight years, I know about budgets and the operational side somewhat, I own my own team — the Tropics. Earl Katz, owner of the 76ers, took all that into consideration, and he feels I can do the job. I will be the first to say that I don't know it all right now, but I am sure willing to learn. I look forward to working with everyone there.

Through all of this I've known that this was another adversity I had to handle sober. I never thought about drinking or using during that time. I kept going to meetings. I talked with my family and close friends. Everything that happened gave me a whole new perspective on things — and it's another example of why I believe that it's so important to keep basketball in perspective. There's a bigger picture here to look at.

Dennis Rodman

I like Lucas because he thinks of his players first and then the game. He is straight. He knows what he knows. He doesn't try to bullshit people, which is good, because in this day and age, you can't. I listen to what he has to say, and when I'd be out walking, it would hit me that something he said really made sense. If he tries to bullshit me or anyone, it will come back to him. Like he always told us, "You can't play both sides of the fence. You can't play on that side and play on this side, too."

It seems that people still remember John as a drug addict, but now his life has totally changed around. John is a good basketball coach, and he did a great job with the Spurs. He got out there and gave a lot. After all the bad things that happened to him, now all the good things are coming to him. If he ever wins the championship, I think his life will feel totally complete. He never won as a player, and he damn sure wants to win as a coach. I think that would mean a lot to him. Oh God, I can't imagine! Then he'd want to win every year!

CHAPTER 10

JOHN LUCAS TODAY

I never realized until starting to do this book just how far back I've come. I really can't believe it. I guess I hadn't sat still long enough to look back. I was too busy, working really hard on myself; all of us who are serious about our recovery work hard on ourselves every day of our lives. It seems that it takes meeting other people who have been watching from the sidelines to tell you where you've come from. All I used to use for a measurement was this: I would say to myself, "Did you drink or use today? No? Then it's been a good day." I may not have played the game, I may not have shot so well, but if I didn't drink, it was a good day. I'm alive.

At this point in my life, I'm using what I call the ABCs of life as my guide. They are based on the Twelve Steps. The first four steps of recovery are basically about acceptance — to *accept* that you're powerless, that you have to surrender. You have to accept that there was some insanity in your life. You have to accept that you must turn your life over to the journey. Although I admitted to having a drug problem in 1980, it took me six more years to really accept it — and acceptance is only the beginning of recovery. Next, you need to *believe* in something greater than yourself to restore some sanity to your life, to relieve those defects and shortcomings. That's in the next four steps. The last four steps are about learning to *care* about other people. And that's my program. I call it the simple ABCs of life. It's the way I live and the way I coach.

I finally made the Hall of Fame. I so badly wanted to make the Hall of Fame of basketball, but I probably won't because of my drug use. No, instead of making the NBA Hall of Fame, I made the Hall of Fame of Drinking and Using. Nobody should have been able to use like I did and survive. I drank and sniffed away jobs and a whole lot of opportunities.

Bob Bass

I've been around this league nearly all my adult life. I've seen a lot of players, and I tell you, John should have been one of the best point guards that ever played in this league. Even though he's not big by NBA standards, he's big enough. He had so much talent and ability, but his drug problem kept him from reaching that level.

People think I could have been an even better player than I was, and they ask me if I regret that. Well, I probably *could* have been a better player if I'd never gotten involved with drugs. But I might not be here to talk about it today — and it's very likely I would have been a shallow person. But life didn't happen that way, and I accept that. I also accept and I'm proud of who I am today.

I can see that for such a long time I've been on a journey to achieve excellence and perfection. Whenever I went out to do something, I went out to do it the very best. I always wanted to achieve a lot, and often I did. Nissalke always used to ask me, "What are you doing, Lucas, running for president?" It was true. I was trying to be everything to everybody because I just wasn't comfortable with who I was. One of the hardest things I had to learn was to like myself. And I think that's one of the things recovery has helped me accomplish. I feel comfortable with me. I like me.

So in a way I have a sense of pride about being in the Hall of Fame of Drinking. It was an expensive price to pay to become eligible for this life, but accepting that I was an alcoholic gave me myself back. All that time I thought I had a great curse, but it was truly a great gift. I don't mind who knows that I'm alcoholic now. That's the A of my ABCs of life — accepting what each day brings for me. I accept life on life's terms, but that's still hard to do sometimes. I've had to accept that I'm getting older, that I'm getting bald, that my hair is getting gray. I've actually looked for a hair weave, but I don't have one because I haven't found one that's good enough. That tells me I still have work to do here.

I've had to learn to accept that my team won't win the NBA championship every year. That my team won't win every game. That I won't be the best coach on the floor every day. That I have to accept others for who they are, too. I have to accept my players for who they are, for the hairstyle they want to wear, everything — I have to accept them and love them unconditionally.

For me there is a lot of pain in recovery. There are a lot of things I have to deal with as a coach, as a friend, as a father, as a husband, as a son, as a person. The way I describe it is to say that there are a lot of things that irritate me, and those irritants are some of the reasons I drank. Part of my challenge in recovery has been to learn how to live and accept life *and* its irritations on a daily basis without isolating myself.

When things used to irritate me, I would isolate myself and go put on some of the saddest music in the world. You know the kind — "My baby done left me, now she's gone." Isolating ourselves is maybe the number-one problem for addicts and alcoholics. When I'd be out on the freeway in the morning stuck in traffic, I'd want to isolate and go get drunk. I had to learn how to handle life's little challenges — like losing a basketball game or having an official not call the game the way I thought it should be called — without isolating and getting drunk. And there are others: getting into a confrontation with a player and feeling I wasn't heard, being unable to trade for a player I wanted, having my kids do the things every day that kids do to irritate you, or even having my father go through surgery in the middle of the season. None of these things are big enough anymore for me to go get drunk or use cocaine.

I've gone through a lot in my life, and while I don't intend to dwell on the past, I will not forget it either because I still remember the pain.

I've had to learn over the last eight years how to live my life with all these irritations without using. And I'm doing it. I'm doing okay.

Sobriety is not my problem, *serenity* is my problem. I'm still learning to let go of the things I can't control. I think people who are goal-oriented like I am can have a particularly tough time with acceptance. We make plans, we set goals, and then we are always trying to control outcomes. Trouble is, you never know what each day holds, and trying to control what you can't just leads to frustration and disappointment.

What's more, I'm still learning to accept that I can't clear away the wreckage of the future. I'm still always trying to figure out how to pick up the pieces of things that haven't even happened yet. I'm learning that I can't always be looking ahead, and when I'm not, then I simply have to accept what comes to me. I have to accept the future; that's what gives me a sense of peace, a feeling of the promises of recovery. When my parents die, that won't be a good enough reason to get drunk. Going bald ain't a good enough reason to get drunk. There *is* no reason that's good enough for me to go get drunk. I can't tell you why I'm going to stay sober today; the challenge for me is to find out what I *do* have to stay sober for on a daily basis. This is really exciting to me.

Each day brings a new challenge of acceptance. What I had to accept last week is often completely different from what I have to accept this week, and that's what's so great about the first four of the Twelve Steps in my life and in the way I live my life — both as a coach and as a person. It's a great pleasure for me to wake up each day to put my sobriety up against life's surprises. I've learned not to push things like I used to do all the time. I try to stay out of God's way and accept the outcomes, the surprises. None of the irritants have been so powerful since March 1986, for me to go and take a drink. Sobriety has won, one day at a time.

The B of my ABCs is believing in something greater than myself. In the past, I truly believed that I was God, and that's because in sports, in school, in anything I wanted to do, I succeeded without ever having to give it a thought. I just did it. My schoolwork, my house, my car, my ideas, my trophies — it all just came to me. I didn't need the Trinity of God. I *was* the Trinity — Me, Myself and I.

But of course, nobody is perfect at everything, and nobody's life goes their way the whole way. When I found out I wasn't perfect as a young man, alcohol and drugs took the pain away. As I got older, and especially after I left Houston, I met some difficulties I didn't know how to handle. I couldn't turn to God because the God I understood then had never helped me before. I thought I was being punished. So I turned more and more to drugs. For me, alcohol and cocaine worked for a while. Think of the sign on a liquor store: wine, beer, and *spirits*. They filled up every empty hole that I had as a young man, as a young adult. Finally I found that alcohol, which was my spirit or my spirituality, just wouldn't work anymore.

When I got into treatment and started attending meetings, I saw people who were just like me. Now if you don't go to Twelve Step meetings, you never see these people who are miracles. Seeing these miracle people started to work on me. I started to believe in something greater than myself. By going all the time, you also find out what happens to some of the people who don't go. They get nothing.

As I dug deeper into the Twelve Step program, I found I could fill my empty holes with a different spirit, and that spirit became my Higher Power, my God. I realized, too, that what the "spirit" alcohol made me feel was only a shell or a weak reflection of what I now feel today as a result of recovery and the Twelve Steps.

This new and true spirit worked more slowly on me, however, than the spirit of alcohol. Alcohol just captured me. Young people, and people I work with in recovery, think you can get spirituality right now. They think it's like ordering a meal from McDonald's. You say "I want it," and you got it. It's not like that. It's a process. It grows in you little by little, day by day.

I learned so much from my drug use. I found out that there's a difference between religiosity and spirituality. Religiosity is often for those people who are afraid to go to hell, and spirituality is for people like me who have already been to hell. I danced with the devil. Now don't misunderstand me here. I don't say this to glorify myself or to brag about how I made it back into the limelight. Remember, I had gotten down so low that people told me I could never ever be in the game of basketball again. When Houston threw me out, they said I would never ever play for them again. So by the time I finally got into recovery, the only thing I wanted was to stop drinking and drugging. Nobody promised me a pot of gold if I quit. I never expected or wanted to be where I am today. All I wanted to do was to stop drinking. That's all. Now tell me, how can there not be a power greater than me?

When I was in treatment, I kept saying, "Why me? Why me? Why did this happen to me?" And a counselor kept saying, "Why not you?! What makes you any different from the next guy?" I thought I was being punished for something, and I can see now that part of the reason for this attitude was that I didn't believe I had a loving God. I saw God as a punishing God. I thought I had used up all my God points. And then I discovered something really amazing. I found out that the God that I knew at a young age, that punishing God, was in fact a loving God. I finally turned in my ego, which had really been getting in the way of my believing in something greater than myself.

Once I started believing in something greater than myself, I found it was easier for me to believe in my players, to believe my friends and family, even to believe in people I don't even know. I don't know a lot of scripture, but I don't think there is anyone who believes in something greater than himself more than I do.

The C of the ABCs is caring about others. Maybe the toughest thing for me to learn in the last few years is to care about people unconditionally. I have had to learn to drop all my prejudices — no matter your color or gender or sexual preference — I had to love you unconditionally. And I do. We are all God's children. I love my players equally. I will do as much for one as I will for the other. I have to be ready to help any alcoholic or addict who really wants help. And I have to forgive. I've mentioned how when I was back playing after treatment some very unkind things were said to me about my drug use. Some people even attacked my kids and my family. I will forgive that. It's not important whether they forgive me or not, but it is important that I forgive them.

I'm very careful to look at my motives when I help people. I want my side of the table to be clean — and that means I am also working to stop putting expectations on others. I don't want to be doing something to get something in return. Particularly when I help famous athletes, I take special care to see that I'm not in the spotlight. I don't need to be in the picture. In fact, I'd prefer no one even know. I don't want people talking about my role. I am just doing what I need to do: I am giving back.

That's one of the reasons I'm doing this book. To give back to others. A number of major publishers wanted me to do a book, but I refused. I struggled a long time about even doing it, because I wanted to make sure my motives were right. And when I finally decided to go ahead, I chose the publisher I did because they are a group of people who know recovery, and I felt they would treat it the right way. I don't really even see this as my autobiography. It's a story within a story that is really about caring for other people. Any proceeds I receive from it will go only to help other people in some way, like paying for someone's treatment. Why? Because I got a free gift. I've discovered that when I try to hoard and keep what I have, then I begin to get frustrated and think I'm not getting what I need — but the more I try to give it away, the more I receive.

In recovery they talk about anonymity all the time, but I've never had the benefit of that. I had to grow up publicly, and that meant I couldn't have any secrets. Everything about me and what I did and what I am today has been in the papers and in other media. But I have so many people around me now to support my recovery. I go to meetings, use the telephone, talk to my players. I have George Gervin, Lloyd Daniels, and Dirk Minniefield. And I have God. We all help each other.

Cheryl Lucas

John seems more at peace with himself. He understands that his life as it is today is a gift to him, and he has a greater appreciation for it than ever before. He's taken something that everybody and their grandmother thought was the worst thing that could ever happen to a person and shown that if you have hope, if you want to turn a negative into a positive, it can be done. But it's your decision and no one else's. Even though he's had a lot of help along the way to get well, it's still John Lucas who did it. And John's a much stronger person for it.

This may sound odd, but I think John's whole drug experience was meant to prepare him for what he's doing now. His drug experience let him know firsthand what it's like to face up to a big problem, to decide it's up to you to do something about it, to be as good as you can and want to be. He learned that no one else can set limits on what you can do and accomplish. You are in charge of that.

In one sense, these drug problems hurt John and our family. It certainly wasn't what we wanted for him. John clearly lost financially because of it, and it may have prevented him from winning a championship as a player. But as it turns out, John won a greater championship: not only was he able to get his life back, he's helping other people get their lives back — and to me, that's the reason we're here. By helping himself, he found that he could help a lot of other people — people he never could have thought he would know or have anything to do with. John loves helping people; if you need his help, he will do anything he can for you. None of the material things really cut it. We can't take them with us. We're here to help other people.

All of us who've been involved in this have been shown that we don't know what plans God has for us, that we aren't really prepared to deal with all the things we end up having to face in life, and that something good can always come out of something that seems to be a burden. That's where the idea of taking each day as it comes is so important. We don't need to think so much about the future because the story does have a happy ending — it's just that we don't know what the end is yet!

John Lucas, Sr.

John has won the hearts and support of people who once treated him in a more perfunctory way. He now commands interest and respect because of the sincerity with which he approaches what he's trying to do. He will do without for someone else. He will even risk his job or his reputation to help someone. He will say no only as a last resort. What's more, I think he has introduced something new to the arena of sports: He is forcing people to begin looking on the players as something more than chattel. Regardless of what others say, he is having an impact.

During the 1993-94 season, I got in a confrontation because I was helping a player from another team — Richard Dumas from the Suns. When I got Richard into my treatment program, his team and some other people in the NBA said my involvement was tampering. They didn't like it that I could talk to him and they couldn't. They called it a conflict of interest.

I got pretty upset about this. I told them — and I'm telling everyone else right now — I'm an alcoholic first. Whenever someone knocks on my door needing help, I will always be there for them. I told the Suns, "If that's ever my son or my daughter knocking at your door, please help them. Don't turn them away." If someone comes to you needing help, then you got to help. It doesn't matter who they are, what race they are, nothing. Go speak to them, then get them help. It's getting the help that counts. Accept the gift. I told them I wouldn't hesitate to do this again. People need to get their priorities in order. Richard's life is far more important that some damn basketball games.

Charles Grantham

Once he became a coach, people began to say that John couldn't be talking to players on other teams because he was now part of management. I will say outright, that's bull-

shit. John's help for Richard was not a conflict of interest. Richard went into the program because he needed to and wanted to. John wasn't trying to sabotage Richard's team or help the Spurs. John isn't calling the shots with the program. John wants to share sobriety and that's what he wants Richard to grab on to. He can't say when Richard comes in and when Richard leaves. He has no control of that. This conflict stuff is so silly. The issue here is sobriety, it's one recovering person trying to help another recovering person. That's what we have to recognize. There are some things that are bigger than the game, and this is one of them.

The most important thing that John has for our players is his sobriety. They need to see it, and those who are struggling and want to share it need to hear how he got it. We have to keep that conflict-of-interest bullshit out of here. We need to make sure that John always has access to any player who is recovering or who needs help.

We have to remember, too, that John is challenged every day. Just like he tells the players who are in the program, he's only one hit away or one drink away. He knows that. Being connected with this program and helping guys like Richard also does good things for John's recovery, so from that perspective, it's a perfect marriage.

John has a unique way of keeping things light while being serious, and that's what makes him not only successful as a coach but as a motivator for those young people who are looking to maintain sobriety.

In the NBA, we've seen the benefit of trying to get to guys early before they get involved with drugs, or at least before their lives get really messed up. That's why I got involved with STAND a few years ago. I don't know how useful it is to tell kids just to not use, or to try to scare them off drugs. Drug use hasn't changed so much in recent years. And when kids are teens, the mentality they have then just makes them want to taste all that forbidden fruit.

As kids grow up they'll make choices about how they live, what they want to do with their lives, and whether or not they're going to use drugs. What I do is tell kids simply to be the best that they can be, and you can't be the best you can be if you use drugs. I've got three kids now — Tarvia, John, and Jai — and with them, I try not to be the parent who says, "Don't do this or that 'cause you'll disgrace the Lucas family name." I just encourage them to be all that they can be. I tell them never to doubt themselves.

I don't know what's going to happen to my kids as far as drugs are concerned. In a way, I wouldn't be surprised if they got involved, because I don't know if heredity plays a role here. Obviously I don't want them to become involved with or addicted to drugs, but I do know that it's possible. I'm living proof that people you never would expect to have a drug problem can have one. There's nothing you can do. That's the God thing. Everybody wants to get up there and say don't do this or that. I say all I can do is try to guide them. All I can do is share my experience with them. Then it's their decision. If they want to go through that thing, well, so be it.

We don't dwell on the subject with the kids. Hell, it's been a long time, and getting longer every day, since I used. They don't even remember much of it. I don't think my son remembers getting in bed with me and telling me to lay my head on his chest and telling me that things were going to be all right. I don't think my daughter remembers pretending to snort ashes.

Tarvia Lucas

With kids my age, yes, there is a problem with drugs. There's a lot of kids who use. I really can't say how many, but I know a lot of them that do. Sometimes I ask them why they do this. Like what's the point of doing it? They say, "Well, I don't drink all the time," but I know they do. But I don't mess with that stuff. I have no intention of using, and I don't let people pressure me. It's just not a good idea to use drugs.

Dad hasn't really said much to me about when he was using drugs, but I know about it. I've been at some of his speeches, so I've heard it, but not from him personally. I don't remember much about that time, except I remember that I got picked on at school. They would call my dad a druggie and stuff like that. But I really didn't let it bother me because I knew who my dad really was. I knew he had a drug problem, but he was my daddy and I loved him either way.

Debbie Lucas

The children don't remember much, but they understand the past. One time we were on a plane going home to North Carolina and a man across from us ordered an alcoholic beverage. John-John said, "Oh, Momma, he's doing drugs. He needs to talk to Dad." So it's there. They know.

To me they were so young then that now it's not weighing that much on them. They see their dad today as an NBA coach. As Tarvia says, "Daddy's got it going on now." That's what they see. They see articles about John's counseling work, his treatment centers, his helping other players — and they really love their daddy.

While I want to give my kids all the tools I can to help them with their lives, I know Debbie and I can't do everything for them. We just have to try to be good parents — and then hope that their teachers do their job and that the other adults who come in contact with my kids are giving them positive direction. And we hope they will make good decisions. Good decisions come through education, through the quality of people they meet, and through a positive structure in their family. Since we're doing that, the only thing left is to trust and have confidence in them.

My kids really like sports, and I tell them that I hope they enjoy athletics. I have no expectations about either one of them becoming a great athlete. I tell them to compete on the court, but to try not to carry that same competition into life. Sports is a great tool to develop skills like concentration and maintaining focus. It's a good thing for that period when you're competing, but you have to remember that once it's over, it's over. I tell them to try to include sports as part of a balanced life, to try to understand that it's just a game. It's not the end, it's only a means to an end. If you put too much pressure on them, they'll miss a heck of a lot of other things in their childhood that they could be enjoying. I really don't put a lot on them about it. I just watch and enjoy them doing it.

Tarvia Lucas

I really enjoy ice skating. I was at this shopping center one day with my mom, watching the skaters, and I knew I wanted to do that. I was only six at the time. My mom always thought it was dangerous, but I got out there and tried it and I just started liking it. Now I practice three hours a day, from 5:30 to 8:30 A.M., five days a week.

The other two sports I enjoy are volleyball and basketball, and those I can do in school. I like playing against different schools and meeting new people. But in ice skating, I put my best foot forward. I plan on going to the 1998 Olympics. I don't know if I'll make it, but that's my goal.

My dad talks to me and my brothers about competition, and he says that if you put your best foot forward and you do well, then you have something to be proud of. If you put your best foot forward and you don't do so well, you still have something to be proud of. I still think the main point is winning, and it's really important to me.

I have to say, though, that while my skating is important, my schoolwork is more important — because I know I can't skate forever. After you accomplish what you can in skating, there's not much to do in it later — and I'm not interested in being a coach. I want to go on to college and get my bach-

elor's and master's degrees. I don't want to be just a skater. Dad knows that I know that school is important, so he really doesn't say much — and besides, I get good grades.

Is winning on the court the most important thing? Is that competitiveness on the court useful in their lives? No, I don't think so. Parents, coaches, and other adults can help build kids' self-esteem. We can give kids love and affection and direction. We can teach them that the goal isn't to win all the time; the goal is to be part of things. When you're on the court, your goal is to give it all you have, but when that hour is over, you stop the competition. Then your goal is to be part of the group.

Kids in sports, like my sons and daughter, will deal with different coaches. I hope people who coach realize what an important role they play in kids' lives. They are like father figures and mother figures to the kids, and I hope that they teach them life skills as well as sport skills. As my kids get older, I see how little control over them I really have, because they are coming into contact with many other people — and they spend less and less time with Debbie and me. This brings me back to trust and love, because I can't shelter them. I put them in an environment, give them a chance to succeed, and hope they do.

Debbie Lucas

John has really taken control of his life. He understands what happened to him when he was young, and how that got him to where he was as an adult — a very competitive person who, at the same time, was trying to please people all the time. I don't think I'm putting pressure on our kids, I think I'm just normal, but John will say I'm pressuring them too much. I think I'm the one now who has to back down from expecting them to be perfect at school. I'm saying that you go to school, you pay attention, you learn, and you do what the teacher tells you do. I expect that, but John reminds me that they're still kids. "They aren't just going to sit there all day and do everything everybody tells them to do," he says.

John's a little bit more relaxed than he used to be, and he's very relaxed with the kids. He says, "Well, when they grow up, especially John, being a guy, they'll have pressure on them because they're black, and more when they start to have a family and have pressure about feeding the kids, getting clothes for them, and putting a roof over their heads. Why put them under more pressure than they need now? Let's try to let them just be kids. They'll have plenty of time to be adults."

I know that as a kid, I didn't put a whole lot of emphasis on my schooling. Fortunately, I did get my degree, and that was a very big help when I finally got sober and got into a life outside of sports. We tell the kids all the time that grades and school are definitely more important than sports. You know kids — they don't always listen, so we had to show that we meant it. We have already stopped John Jr. once from playing because his grades weren't good enough. Basketball is not why he is in school. No matter how good he is, if he can't do what is required to be a member of his class, he'll never be able to do it in his occupation — and that's no good. We told him, "If you want to be a member of the team, then you better find the desire to get your grades up, too." I tell him all the time, "It will work if you want it."

John Lucas, Jr.

I play basketball, tennis, and hockey. I do a lot of sports because they keep me busy. It's fun to play. You meet more people and make more friends. I like to win, too, but I say, "If we win, we win, and if we don't, we don't." Because you cannot win everything. My dad talks to me about this. He says that if you lose, just keep your head. He says that the most important thing is that you play. All that's important to me in sports is basketball. It's my favorite. But I know I got to study, too.

My dad's talked to me about drugs, and he's said not to do it, that drugs can mess up anybody's life. They are bad for you. And he said not to hang with the wrong kind of group. I do see some kids my age that use, like drink sometimes. But I wouldn't use anything.

I would like to be a professional athlete, but if anything happens that I can't, I'd rather run my dad's business.

I realize that I don't have any secrets anymore — my recovery has been very public. I was afraid to go back and play basketball. I didn't know if I could do it and stay sober. What's more, I let some people put more pressure and fear on me when they said that I would hurt the name of recovery because I had failed before — and I might slip again. Fortunately, some good people helped me see that it wasn't fair to put that on me. And they were right. I know that I am an example of recovery for a lot of people — people who have probably never heard of Alcoholics Anonymous, the Twelve Steps, or the Big Book (*Alcoholics Anonymous,* the textbook for the fellowship of the same name).

It's important that I share my experience because that experience might give them some of the strength and hope they need. That's all that matters. I'm no different than anyone else. I care about people — a lot. I won't be the last Spurs or 76ers coach. No team will die without me. And recovery won't die without me, either. If I choose to drink and have a slip, recovery won't die and it won't mean recovery doesn't work. It only means I chose to drink. It means that I had a slip; it means that for that moment, sobriety lost its priority. That's all.

Joyce Bossett

John has finally arrived. He's his own person now — very serene, with an inner peace. He doesn't get as excited as he used to. He's aware of and understands his feelings. He knows how to take advantage of adversity. When things are tough today, he basically says, "You have to leave it to God.

*It's out of my hands." He used to think he could fix every-
thing, but now he sees that there's a master plan. He is no
longer ashamed of his past, and he understands why he is
here.*

*Lucas was given a gift from God that he should cherish.
He's surrounded by people who love him, and he's received
a second chance on life and exposure to another way of living. He's really very lucky. John understands that life is solid,
not fluff, and that it's important to make a contribution. One of
his favorite sayings is "I've got to give it away to keep it." He
says, "I have to know that I'm not ignoring my fellow man.
Others took a chance on me and I'll never forget that. I have
an obligation to help other people in the same way." He's
very sincere about this work; he's not just paying lip service
to it.*

*The nice thing about John is that he does these things
that you don't know about. At the hospital once, we had a
family whose home had burned down. So someone started a
community fund drive to help them get clothes and so on.
One day I heard that they had gotten a lot of money, but they
had no idea from whom. A bit later, I ran into John and mentioned it. Then I saw this bit of a smile on his face, and I said,
"You did that, didn't you!" And he did.*

*What does the future hold for John? Though he likes
coaching very much, John talks sometimes about being the
coaching for only a few more years and then going back to
his "real life and love," which, he says, is treatment. I think he
will find a way to balance these two loves for the time being
and have the best of both worlds.*

*I think John will stay in coaching. He will work to upgrade
the health care component for the NBA, and then take what
he's done for the NBA to other professional sports. John
would love to get into the hockey and football leagues. He
has a strong interest in baseball, too, from a treatment stand-
point. He feels that they have never really had a formalized*

way to deal with these problems, and he'd like to be involved in creating some of that. Being an NBA coach would give him the visibility and the leverage to get in those doors.

Coaching is a very stressful job, and John's found it a lot lonelier than he thought. John is the kind of guy who does well when he's surrounded by people who offer him unconditional love. He really misses his family. It's not unusual for people to ask me, is coaching good for him? does it create too much risk? is it too stressful for him? Only John can tell, but I think that if anybody can stay sober, he can, because sobriety is a priority in his life and he works on it all the time.

Recently I heard him speak, and he told the audience that I was responsible for rescuing him. John gives me much more credit than I deserve. I told him afterwards, "John, you have worked your sobriety. You are the reason you are sober. I just happened to be able to give you a support network when you needed one. That's what treatment services are all about."

I think there's something in John Lucas that he's still struggling with, and he hasn't quite put his finger on it. There are times when I see a sad overcast on his face. I don't know if it's regret over the years he wasted with drugs or what. I remember a very bad time in my office when we were playing back an interview he'd done on CNN. He looked quite depressed, and I said, "John, what's wrong?" "Just look at me," he said, "I look awful." I told him I thought he looked fine, but he said, "I look years older than I am. The drugs just really beat me up and I guess I had to get sober to notice it."

I think he's struggling with where he wants to be emotionally and spiritually. Those are big problems to be working on, and not uncommon ones for someone his age, either. When you're thirty-five or forty, you begin to realize that you have lived awhile and that you aren't going to live forever. You see that you can't do everything you want to in one lifetime, so you have to decide what's really important and what

you really want to do. John thinks about these things a lot.
The reality of death is hitting him.

Coaching the Spurs was something I did for me. And you know, even though I still complain about some things — like my gray hair — *I like me today.* I am by no means perfect, but I'm making progress. I have more today than I ever had: I have unconditional love from my family, and I have learned to love myself, shortcomings and all.

I'm just another alcoholic trying to stay sober. I'm just trying to do the next thing that God gives me to do. Basketball and tennis are what I did, but this is who I am. I'm a grateful addict/alcoholic. "Coach" is just a title. My primary purpose in life is to try to help other recovering addicts. Beyond that, I'm just trying to be the best John Lucas I can be, and that takes so much effort that I don't try to deal with everything that's going on. I just take what comes next and then let it go — that's what they mean by living one day at a time.

I know my experience isn't unique. There are other athletes who have gone through similar struggles, gone through times like I did. But some of them found when they got out of sports that they didn't have anything else to do. A lot of guys who've been in sports and through treatment are really angry. I'm not angry about what happened to me. If I had to do it all over again, I'd do it the same way — *if* I knew I would be the person I am today. I'd be really afraid of having to go through all that pain again, but I would. It took all of that to kill some of the ego that I developed over the years. I'm grateful that I didn't get what I was asking for, doing all those drugs — I could be dead. But I'm not: Recovery saved my life. When I look at it this way, I truly have no regrets. What I always thought was a curse — addiction — has in fact turned out to be the greatest gift I've ever been given. My addiction carried me past my sports life. It gave me my best trophy. It gave me John Lucas. It gave me life.

GEORGE "ICEMAN" GERVIN

Considered the greatest player in Spurs history, George Gervin scored 23,602 points and set virtually every club scoring record during his twelve years with the team. He ranks eighth in professional basketball in total points with 26,595, and his NBA scoring average of 26.2 points per game ranks seventh on the all-time list. He held the Spurs single-game scoring record — 63 points — until 1994 when David Robinson scored 70 in the final game of the season.

The Iceman played in twelve straight All Star games — from 1974 to 1985 — and was named the game's MVP in 1980 when he had 34 points and 10 rebounds. Gervin was All-NBA first team five times, All-NBA second team twice, and one of just three players in NBA history (along with Michael Jordan and Wilt Chamberlain) to win four or more scoring titles. His streak of 407 straight games in double figures is the fourth longest in NBA history. (Note: George Gervin's comments were recorded in the spring of 1994, when John Lucas was the head coach of the Spurs.)

John and I, we go way back. We go way back beyond teammates and playing together in San Antonio, living that same lifestyle of going fast and playing good basketball. I felt his love for the game was just as great as mine. That's really what makes basketball players special — when they really love it and it's not just for the money or the glory, but it's for the work that you put into it. That puts me close to a person when they're like that because I feel we are one and the same. Talent doesn't matter; it's the desire to play the game, and that was the greatest part I liked about John.

That's how John was. He was always energetic, too, no matter what we did. He'd be the loudest one, the one doing all the talking, the one doing all the hollering, the one saying check off, the one talking trash. That was him.

Even when he was playing with Houston and I was with San Antonio, we had a rivalry. He'd always be saying, "I'm going to kill you today, Ice, I'm shutting you out." One night we played Houston for back to back games. I stayed up all night before the first game getting high, so I was all drained going into the game. I only got six points, and John, he was shouting, "I held Ice to six, I held Ice to six."

I got pretty pissed. I mean I was really mad. We played them the next day and I got 46 and we beat them. I went back and told him, "I told you, you didn't stop me last night, what I did the night before stopped me." John just started laughing because I blew him out of the gym. We still laugh about this today.

John and I were together when he was going downhill. We used to get high together, but at that time, he was a little further gone than I was. His tolerance had pretty much reached its peak, but mine wasn't there yet. John used to use so much that he couldn't come to practice the next day. Now me, I used to get high and I'd still come. He'd go and miss, and I'd say, "Man, why you go stay up all night and then not come to practice? They're going to find out."

I didn't understand why he did that, but I found out soon enough. I just hadn't got to John's point yet. But I did. Cocaine eventually just took me over the edge, too. John just reached his limit a little sooner. Now John's always had some good traits, but when he was using, oh my, but he was wild and crazy. He was so hyper, he wouldn't even sit down. He wasn't using his common sense or the intellect we found out later he really has. He was just a young boy in a fantasy world, just like me.

When, I saw John go down, I said, "No, that ain't *never* going to happen to me." Hell, I was hooked up in the same world that most kids are in today. They see their friends going down from drugs, but yet they'll say, "It can't happen to me." Well, I was one of those saying it couldn't happen to me. Shit, I just didn't know.

John and I were together during our non-sober days, and we got close. At the time, we thought maybe it was the drugs, but really it was fate that we got together. What really counts to me about John — and this came after basketball — is he helped save my life. I was heading down that road of destruction, and I really needed someone to look up to in dealing with the problems that I was having. I didn't really have a role model, and John helped me stop.

It was after he straightened up his life, when he'd started his comeback and gotten his program started, that I saw for myself how he was turning his life around. This gave me hope, and I said, "Hey man, I see this SOB can come out." He made something out of his life and that really inspired me. So I believed in what he was teaching. He was teaching people how to live again. And I wanted to live again.

I overdosed on cocaine in 1988. I was in the hospital with my blood pressure 260 over 70. The doctors really wondered why I wasn't dead. But I knew I was in God's hands and beyond the help of man. It was *fate.* Once I survived, my wife and family called John. He came and took me down to his treatment center in Houston.

Of course I was fighting it for the first few days, like most of us addicts do. I felt that once I was in there three or four days, I didn't need no more goddamn treatment. I felt that I was well, so I wanted to come out. I used to fight with John and I'd say, "I don't want to stay in this SOB." But that was the drugs really coming out of me, and once I stayed a few more days, all the drugs was out of me and then I had to deal with my behavior.

That's another place where he took control. You see, I'm an athlete and I felt, "Shit, I'll do what I want, I'm different. You guys ain't got the same story I got, and I can't tell you sons of bitches all my secrets." That's the attitude I had — not understanding that we're all basically the same (except I'm just taller) and that the drug basically does everybody the same way.

John had the right treatment. I was afraid to really show my inner self to other people. I used to say, "I'm going to write a book, John, and if I tell these people everything now, they're going to know my book." You know what John would say? He'd laugh at me and say, "Ice, we ain't no different than nobody else. We may think we are, but that man had the same problem you got."

That's why I believe in the program. All of us, we're basically the same. All the guidance and direction eventually has to come from inside you, because the true test is when you're outside the facility and you're really ready to go fight that demon head on.

When I got through with my forty days in Luke's place, I was afraid to go back out because I really didn't want to go back and live like I lived. I almost destroyed my family, and my kids were scared of me. I knew that wasn't the way for me. So I stayed there in Houston, away from my family, for another ninety days in the aftercare program. I stayed with Luke all that time. He used to come and get me every morning at 6:00, and we'd go train for an hour, an hour and a half. Then I'd go to my group meetings and afterward we'd go play ball.

Since it was his treatment center, John had his own agenda. And since he'd been through it, he felt that this agenda would work for other athletes. He was right. John got me to jump through a hoop that I never thought I could. And that's something for me, because I'm a strong-willed, kind of egotistical person, so you can't hardly tell me shit. I won't listen to you. But John had always felt like a kind of older brother for me, and he opened the door for me. I swear it was fate. It was part of our destinies that this happened like it did. Because I never had nobody I could turn to and I ain't never trusted nobody, but I trusted John. John got me through that hoop. There was nothing he could have told me to do that I wouldn't have done it, because John matured through his recovery and he got a lot of wisdom. He taught me that there isn't any substance to this kind of life unless you have some spirituality. If you're one of those guys who's anxious to see the world, there's a lot for you to see playing in this league — and you can get caught up out there while you're looking. That's what happened to me and John.

In the middle of the 1992-93 season, John gets the job with San Antonio. At the time, I'd been doing community relations for them for three years already. I knew the owner, Red McCombs, real well, and one day he called me into a meeting about the Coach Tarkanian situation. He mentioned some ideas he had, and John was one of them.

After that meeting, I ran straight home and called John and said, "John, Red down here mentioned your name in the same sentence as these other coaches to take over the Spurs. What's this?" John laughed and said, "Oh, Ice, it probably ain't nothing." But John knew all the time because they had already talked. The next day, he gets the job, and that night John's at the arena. He sees me and just starts laughing. He said to me, "Ice, I couldn't let you know," and I said, "John, you *are* a son of a bitch!"

The next day at John's first practice, Red and I were sitting up in the stands when John walked out of the locker room onto the floor. He called up to me, "Ice! I want you down here with me tomorrow at practice. I'll get someone to get your stuff. I want you to help me coach." Well here I am with this community relations job, sitting in the stands with the owner. When John said that, I was so nervous because you know nobody don't get a job that way.

That night, John flew back to Houston to get his stuff, so I called him at home. I said, "John, now what do you want me to do tomorrow?" He said, "I want you on the floor to help me to coach." I said, "Really, really?" And he says in that voice of his, "Yeah, Ice, just be there tomorrow." He knew that I was nervous, and I was, but I came there the next day and I was a coach.

As coach, I know my role. It's to guard John's back; I want him to do and be the best he can as a coach. If I see something that he needs to address, no matter what it is, he knows I'll bring it up to him. I ain't scared of him, and I ain't worried about losing my job. Maybe some things I say he won't like, but I don't give a crap. If I feel it's the best for him and the team or even his family, I'm going to tell him because he's my friend.

The greatest gift I have to give to this team is tradition. I was one of the superstars of the game, and guys remember me because I was a true entertainer. Guys respect you for that. And then I have this ability to deal with people. That's why John calls me the chemistry coach. I work with the chemistry. I keep the camaraderie going. I play around with the guys, and John lets me do that. He knows I can still play, and guys are more apt to listen to you if you can demonstrate and show them versus just tell them. Now I'm not interested in a head coaching job. I really want to be by John's side.

I know he's capable of being a superstar coach because he's got the gift to communicate and be understood. He has experienced a lot, so he's got stories to tell, and he uses them to get his points across. You see, this game is played with people, and if you can get them to understand that all of you are working toward the same objective, you're going to be successful. Being an ex-player, John knows that you have to have pride in what you're doing as a team in order to take it to the next level. He's helped them understand that. To do that takes a true leader, and John is a natural leader. Plus, I want to help John keep his hair — I want that bald spot to stay just that size it is today.

You know, John's coaching Dennis Rodman. Now most coaches in the league will say, "I couldn't coach him," or "I couldn't let him do the things he's doing." I mean, what is he doing? He's getting twenty, twenty-five rebounds every night. It takes an intelligent man to deal with a personality like Dennis Rodman because Dennis is a special guy. I love him, I think he's a beautiful guy. I think he's real sensitive. He's very physical and strong, and I think he uses that sometimes to cover up his sensitivity. But John understands that, and Dennis understands John.

I always say that John is the coach of the 1990s, because the kids we are dealing with, well, he's able to deal with them. He can talk their language and relate to them, and that's how he's able to get the best out of them. A lot of these coaches around this league are going to find out how important the relationship with your guys really is.

John says that coaching is just a hobby. Hell, I just *love* it when he says that. A hobby! People might misunderstand that or get mad and say it isn't a hobby, it's a job." John's bigger than that. John helps save *lives.* They might worry about making a dollar, but John helps save lives. There ain't no greater gift than that, man. Only the Creator is more powerful than someone trying to help somebody.